Praise for *Keep Your Head Up*

"Anticipatory grief can feel messy and isolating. But in *Keep Your Head Up*, Tasha Faruqui manages to paint her devastatingly beautiful journey with relatable strokes—reminding us all that even while staring down grief, there is so much life to live."

—Kelly Cervantes,
USA TODAY bestselling author of *Normal Broken*

"In *Keep Your Head Up*, Dr. Faruqui speaks openly about some of the lesser-known aspects of parenting a child with medical complexity, including mental health issues, spirituality, sibling experiences, parental dreams and expectations, and learning to embrace an unexpected path. Readers of any background will find something in this book that resonates with them."

—K. Jane Lee,
MD, author of *Catastrophic Rupture: A Memoir of Healing*

"Tasha Faruqui's memoir *Keep Your Head Up* is a story of becoming. Who we chose to be, and who life requires us to become. In this beautiful pager turner, the reader is left breathless by what life and parenting can truly ask of us. This beautifully written book offers so many often-left unsaid truths about grief and loss written plainly on the page, gifting us a deep understanding of what it means to be wholly human in the most deeply spiritual way."

—Meghan Riordan Jarvis,
Trauma and grief therapist, author of
Can Anyone Tell Me: Essential Questions About Grief & Loss

"Parents, providers, and caregivers will find themselves deeply seen in these pages. With the heart of a mother and the insight of a physician, Dr. Faruqui shows us how to live and love even in life's most uncertain terrain."

—Kacie Gikonyo,
RN, Death Doula, and founder of Death Doula School™

KEEP YOUR HEAD UP

KEEP YOUR HEAD UP

A Mother's Story of Chasing Joy
in the Face of Grief

TASHA FARUQUI, DO

Copyright © 2025 by Wiley. All rights reserved.

Published by John Wiley & Sons, Inc., Hoboken, New Jersey.Published simultaneously in Canada.

No part of this publication may be reproduced, stored in a retrieval system, or transmitted in any form or by any means, electronic, mechanical, photocopying, recording, scanning, or otherwise, except as permitted under Section 107 or 108 of the 1976 United States Copyright Act, without either the prior written permission of the Publisher, or authorization through payment of the appropriate per-copy fee to the Copyright Clearance Center, Inc., 222 Rosewood Drive, Danvers, MA 01923, (978) 750-8400, fax (978) 750-4470, or on the web at www.copyright.com. Requests to the Publisher for permission should be addressed to the Permissions Department, John Wiley & Sons, Inc., 111 River Street, Hoboken, NJ 07030, (201) 748-6011, fax (201) 748-6008, or online at http://www.wiley.com/go/permission.

The manufacturer's authorized representative according to the EU General Product Safety Regulation is Wiley-VCH GmbH, Boschstr. 12, 69469 Weinheim, Germany, e-mail: Product_Safety@wiley.com.

Trademarks: Wiley and the Wiley logo are trademarks or registered trademarks of John Wiley & Sons, Inc. and/or its affiliates in the United States and other countries and may not be used without written permission. All other trademarks are the property of their respective owners. John Wiley & Sons, Inc. is not associated with any product or vendor mentioned in this book.

Limit of Liability/Disclaimer of Warranty: While the publisher and the authors have used their best efforts in preparing this work, including a review of the content of the work, neither the publisher nor the authors make any representations or warranties with respect to the accuracy or completeness of the contents of this work and specifically disclaim all warranties, including without limitation any implied warranties of merchantability or fitness for a particular purpose. No warranty may be created or extended by sales representatives, written sales materials or promotional statements for this work. The fact that an organization, website, or product is referred to in this work as a citation and/or potential source of further information does not mean that the publisher and authors endorse the information or services the organization, website, or product may provide or recommendations it may make. This work is sold with the understanding that the publisher is not engaged in rendering professional services. The advice and strategies contained herein may not be suitable for your situation. You should consult with a specialist where appropriate. Further, readers should be aware that websites listed in this work may have changed or disappeared between when this work was written and when it is read. Neither the publisher nor authors shall be liable for any loss of profit or any other commercial damages, including but not limited to special, incidental, consequential, or other damages.

For general information on our other products and services or for technical support, please contact our Customer Care Department within the United States at (800) 762-2974, outside the United States at (317) 572-3993 or fax (317) 572-4002.

Wiley also publishes its books in a variety of electronic formats. Some content that appears in print may not be available in electronic formats. For more information about Wiley products, visit our web site at www.wiley.com.

Library of Congress Cataloging-in-Publication Data is Available:

ISBNs: 9781394358762 (Hardback)
ISBNs: 9781394358786 (ePDF)
ISBNs: 9781394358779 (ePub)

COVER DESIGN: PAUL MCCARTHY
COVER IMAGE: © ADOBE STOCK | BERKAYO8

SKY10122970_072625

*To my Soraya: may the world hear your two wise thoughts:
Anyone with disabilities should not be made fun of because
these special needs are their superpowers.
You never know what someone is going through.*

Contents

	Prologue: Boulevard of Broken Dreams	*xi*
	Chapter Playlist	*xv*
1	**Waving Through a Window**	**1**
2	**Send Me on My Way**	**9**
3	**Perfect**	**17**
4	**Take the Power Back**	**27**
5	**Nothing Better**	**35**
6	**Father of Mine**	**41**
7	**Follow You into the Dark**	**47**
8	**Welcome to Your Life**	**57**
9	**It's Quiet Uptown**	**65**
10	**Cherub Rock**	**73**
11	**Ways to Go**	**81**
12	**Nuthin' but a "G" Thang**	**87**
13	**Fix You**	**93**
14	**Underwater**	**99**
15	**All I Need**	**105**
16	**Vindicated**	**113**

17	**I Still Haven't Found What I'm Looking For**	**121**
18	**Float On**	**127**
19	**The 7th Element**	**137**
20	**Mr. Brightside**	**141**
21	**The World Has Turned and Left Me Here**	**147**
22	**Sleepyhead**	**153**
23	**Just Breathe**	**161**
24	**False Confidence**	**169**
25	**Good Life**	**175**
26	**Home**	**181**
27	**Pompeii**	**187**
28	**Riptide**	**191**
29	**Don't Give Up on Me**	**197**
30	**Time of Your Life**	**205**
31	**Landslide**	**209**
32	**Take Me to Church**	**217**
33	**Let Me In**	**225**
34	**Another Life**	**231**
	Conclusion: Take This Ride	*237*
	Acknowledgments	*241*
	About the Author	*243*
	Index	*245*

Prologue
Boulevard of Broken Dreams

"Is this happening faster than you'd imagined?" he asked.

At a recent appointment, my daughter Soraya's palliative care doctor led our conversation in a more philosophical direction than usual.

My mind—and heart—started racing. Why is he bringing this up? What is he really trying to say? Is this really the beginning of the end?

Because, yes, things were progressing faster than we thought when we started seeing him a year ago. Soraya's regimen now included medication to help manage her increasing pain. She relied on her ventilator all night, and sometimes during the day, too. She was using her wheelchair almost full-time. Exhaustion was the norm.

Instead of answering directly, though, I flipped the question back on him. "Do *you* think it is?"

Even though I am a doctor, it didn't stop me from believing Soraya's care team may have magically discovered something to help her live longer or experience less pain. It doesn't mean I'm beyond hoping for a miracle, even though everything she's been through— everything we've been through as a family—over the past 11 years tells me the picture I keep trying to manifest won't be the one that develops.

Beyond anything else in this situation, I'm simply a mom who would do anything for her daughter. Even though science has failed us when it comes to finding a cure or even a diagnosis for her, I still hold out hope we may yet find an effective treatment or even just a reprieve from this steady decline. Hope is about the only thing I have to hold onto these days. It's my life preserver in a sea of unanswered questions and sunken dreams.

"I'm going to be purposely vague here," he replied, as calm and kind and unflappable as ever. "If we look at her function from last summer to now, I would say there has been quite a significant change. However, she's not on her vent all day and we're only dipping our toes in the shallow end of the pool in terms of pain meds, so in that regard, things are going fairly well."

Translation: this kind, caring doctor hadn't suddenly become omniscient. He had no idea what, when, why, or how Soraya's health would change from here on out, just like every other specialist and subspecialist we'd consulted over the years, of which there had been multitudes. Even the National Institutes of Health had no idea what the problem was, no less have an answer for it, so there was no need to think anything would change now.

Still, there was some good news hidden within his message: I felt validated that things were, in fact, as I was seeing them. His metaphor about remaining in the shallow end of the pool, for the moment, felt gently reassuring. His openness and honesty were incredibly refreshing.

"So many of the families I work with are living parallel lives," he continued. "One is in the grieving, and the other is in keeping up with the day-to-day reality of caring for a sick child. They're so focused on the past and what they think they should have done, or worrying about the future and what might happen, that they're never actually present. I just want you to know I think you're doing a great job of adapting to the changes in Soraya's condition while still living in the moment."

It certainly hadn't been easy, but I felt the truth in his words. Over the past year, we'd shifted as a family, from going on big bucket list trips to finding ways to spend time together that didn't involve going anywhere far, or even anywhere at all. We'd had the big, hard, emotional conversations. We'd learned to voice our concerns and frustrations along with our joys and victories, both large and small. Everyone—including Soraya—knew the status of her health and the eventual outcome.

We were, in almost every way, your typical, average family. That is, with one major exception: my middle child was dying, and there wasn't a damn thing anyone could do about it.

Dear Reader . . .

This book was intended for parents of children with complex medical needs. However, when I've shared passages of the manuscript with others, I've been delighted to learn how much it resonates with audiences far beyond just those with an interest in medically complex children. Physicians and health professionals, who often only have 15 minutes to spend with patients, say it has provided them with a guide for how to have the most impact in that short amount of time. Parents of special needs children tell me it has made them feel more understood and less alone. Parents of healthy, neurotypical kids feel it mirrors their quest for wanting only the best for their children. I truly believe that any reader can find some element of this book to relate to.

Being a pediatrician and parent I found myself in a place where I had a unique perspective that I could share as we look at Soraya's care. There were experiences that I had that I could not refer to in a medical textbook or a parenting textbook. Similarly, there was no "village" or support groups that I could lean into. If I was struggling in isolation—and I had the privilege of having the education being a trained physician—what were other parents doing to survive their daily routines? When Soraya entered hospice, I struggled even more

xiii

Prologue

with the question: how do I live life knowing my daughter is dying? I truly felt that I needed to put the pain and struggle into purpose, so I wrote this book.

This book covers more than a parenting story; it begins with the story of my life. It's important to know the person I was and the dreams that I carried for my adulthood. It's important to know that there were struggles in my life that led me to believe that I could not endure any more challenges. There was the fallacy that getting through medical school would be the *last* challenge of my life.

On a more personal note, music helped me through many challenges in my life. In the periods of transition, hardship, and joy, music has been a part of it. Each chapter title is either a direct song title or a part of a lyric in a song that has a significant memory attached to it. I hope putting it all together will give the reader insight into the playlist of my life.

I hope that anyone that has a dream or plan—and then grieves the loss of that plan—will read this book. May it help you feel less alone and more connected with others.

Chapter Playlist

Prologue: *Boulevard of Broken Dreams,* Green Day

1. *Waving Through a Window,* Ben Platt and Original Broadway Cast of Dear Evan Hansen

2. *Send Me on My Way,* Rusted Root

3. *Perfect,* P!nk

4. *Take the Power Back,* Rage Against the Machine

5. *Nothing Better,* The Postal Service

6. *Father of Mine,* Everclear

7. *Follow You into the Dark,* Death Cab for Cutie

8. *Welcome to Your Life,* Grouplove

9. *It's Quiet Uptown,* From Broadway Musical *Hamilton*

10. *Cherub Rock,* The Smashing Pumpkins

11. *Ways to Go,* Grouplove

12. *Nuthin' but a "G" Thang,* Dr. Dre

13. *Fix You,* Coldplay

14. *Underwater,* Rüfüs Du Sol

15. *All I Need,* Radiohead

16. *Vindicated,* Dashboard Confessional

17. *Still Haven't Found What I Am Looking For,* U2

18. *Float On,* Modest Mouse

19. *The 7th Element,* Vitas

20. *Mr. Brightside,* The Killers

21. *The World Has Turned and Left Me Here,* Weezer

22. *Sleepyhead,* Passion Pit

23. *Just Breathe,* Telepopmusik

24. *False Confidence,* Noah Kahan

25. *Good Life,* One Republic

26. *Home,* Phil Phillips

27. *Pompeii,* Bastille

28. *Riptide,* Vance Joy

29. *Don't Give Up on Me,* Andy Grammer

30. *Good Riddance (Time of Your Life),* Green Day

31. *Landslide,* Fleetwood Mac/The Smashing Pumpkins

32. *Take Me to Church,* Hozier

33. *Let Me In,* Grouplove

34. *Another Life,* Rufus Du Sol

Conclusion: *Take This Ride,* Vigiland

Chapter 1

Waving Through a Window

Looking back, there have been three major themes in my life: **expectations** (both those placed on me and those I've projected onto my future), **fierce independence** (despite what was expected of me), and **fitting in** (or not). In my more myopic moments, I see these as a direct result of being the child of immigrants, but when I zoom out, I can appreciate that, while the journey has been specifically mine, the feelings are universal. After all, who *doesn't* bristle at the expectations of others, believe their lives "should" go a certain way, long to express their authentic selves, and yearn for belonging? I'd venture to say every single one of us does. That's humanity for you.

My story starts, I suppose, when my mom emigrated from Bangladesh at 16, arriving in the United States with a limited education, even more limited English skills, and a new husband she barely knew. In our culture, it's common to get married at an early age—my grandmother was married at 12 and my aunt at 14—so my mom was just following tradition. In opposition to it, though, she'd entered into a "love" marriage instead of having an arranged one, the only one of the six kids in her family to do so. Let's just say their "love" didn't last long.

Mom married him because he'd kissed her on the cheek. Having no knowledge otherwise, she thought that kiss meant she was going to get pregnant—and if they were having a child, she'd better become his wife. As you might imagine, it wasn't the best foundation for a long-term relationship.

By 17, she gave birth to my sister. By 21, she had me. And by the time she was 26, my dad dropped the three of us from Mississippi to Illinois to my uncle's house, told her he wanted a divorce, and walked out of our lives. He left us essentially homeless and with only two weeks' worth of clothing.

Thankfully, my uncle offered to let us stay with him and his family while my mom took odd jobs and tried to save money to get us a place of our own. She worked as a waitress. A babysitter. A nursing assistant. A garment maker. We all slept in the same room, in the same bed.

After two years, she'd earned enough to move us into a decent apartment located in a Community Housing project. As much as she appreciated her brother's help, my mom wanted to prove she could make it on her own. That meant working more hours than ever, along with taking night classes at the community college. It wasn't the best recipe for being a mother to two young girls, but it would have to do.

A stream of less-than-reliable babysitters followed, and my sister and I were often left to our own devices. By kindergarten, I had my own key to our place and knew to walk myself to the bus stop when Bozo's grand prize game started on TV. Mom had already drilled into our little heads that we needed an education, so we'd always be able to stand on our own feet, and I never lingered longer despite missing the exciting ending of the show because I understood school was of the utmost importance.

I also understood that our situation was unique, and I started feeling like a live action version of that song on *Sesame Street*: "One of these things is not like the others." My friends never had to live in their uncle's house or share a bed with their mother and sister.

They were escorted to the bus stop instead of walking alone, signaled by a certain segment of a TV show. In kindergarten, I was told to watch *The Bozo Show* and when Bozo (the clown) introduced "The Grand Prize Game" that was my cue to turn off the TV, lock the door, and go to my bus stop. The contrast remained for after school as well, where other children were let into their houses instead of letting themselves in with a key attached to their backpack. They always had a parent home, or at the very least a dependable babysitter, instead of being on their own or left with random people who might or might not show up on any given day.

For obvious reasons, the local Bangladeshi community started pushing my mom to find a new husband. Their view was *You're a single woman with no college education. You have two kids and you're dirt poor, so you need to find somebody to take care of you.* Family, friends, and friends of friends scoured their contacts for eligible bachelors.

They soon located a single surgeon who lived in rural Michigan. It was considered a perfect match for many reasons: first, he was also from Bangladesh, although he'd grown up in a small village as opposed to a city like my mom. Second, as the eldest son in his family, he'd taken on financial responsibility for his 10 siblings and their children(!) after his father died, so his fiscal life was in order. Finally, and probably most important, he was divorced, and he needed someone who would understand and accept his situation—maybe even someone who'd found herself in the *same* situation.

On coming to the States, he fell in love with an American nurse who was both Caucasian and Christian (unlike him, my mom, my bio dad, and most people from Bangladesh, who are Muslim). They got married, had three children, and then divorced when she cheated on him. Worried about his newly wifeless status, his family quickly arranged for a second marriage with a woman from his village in

3

Waving Through a Window

Bangladesh. This second wife found living in the rural United States more isolating than she could handle, so they promptly divorced, and she went back home.

Although he was still considered an extremely eligible bachelor due to his status as a physician, he was hesitant to marry another woman from Bangladesh, knowing how difficult the cultural transition had been for his second wife. Ideally, he wanted to find a traditional Bangladeshi woman who already lived in America. Enter my mom.

Being Bangladeshi, Muslim, divorced, and in the Midwest, my mom ticked every box as a potential new spouse for him. Everyone decided it was an ideal partnership, despite the 18 years separating them—my mom was 28 and he was 46 at the time—so they talked a bit over the phone, then met in person at a community picnic. I remember running up to him that day and asking if I could call him Dad. He, of course, said yes, and from then on, he's always been Dad to me. Although love at first sight would be something of an overstatement, if you asked him today, he'd tell you he fell in love as soon as he saw me and my sister. It also doesn't hurt that my mother is beautiful.

As for Mom, it was almost like she reverted from love marriage to an arranged marriage. This wasn't a foreign concept, and it seemed to work for a lot of people in our culture. She knew she'd made a mistake the first time around and was willing to sacrifice anything and everything to make our lives better. Besides, she could see positive characteristics in Dad that my biological father hadn't possessed, like a good job, a good head on his shoulders, and a willingness to be a loving father who actually enjoyed the role. To be honest, she also appreciated that he was a physician who owned a house and had all sorts of things that we didn't at the time.

It was a done deal. They got married, my sister and I got a new father, and we all got a new lease on life. As for our biological father, he made increasingly rare appearances after that. Most of our scheduled supervised visitations ended up being playdates with my uncle because bio dad never showed up. He once started a custody battle with my mom but then barely attended any of the hearings. Before long, my sister and I came to understand that we shouldn't ask to see or even mention bio dad because it would be disrespectful and hurtful to our new dad.

A giant perk of our new life was that Dad was much more "Americanized" than Mom. Instead of using the Bengali words *Abbu*, *Amma*, and *Apa* for father, mother, and sister, we now used the American terms. We ate with utensils instead of using our hands. Dad stocked root beer (so cool! pop!) in the fridge for me and my sister, and my mom tried her first sip of alcohol—a glass of wine on their honeymoon. My much older stepbrothers and stepsister were being raised Christian, so we celebrated Christmas and Easter along with Ramadan. I was thrilled. As a kid you don't want to be different; you want to assimilate. I assimilated quickly.

In Dowagiac, Michigan, Dad was one of two doctors in our new hometown of less than 6,000 people. He practiced as both a family practitioner and surgeon, doing everything from annual exams and sick visits to total hip replacements, C-sections, and appendectomies. Essentially, his services ran the gamut from birth to death. If patients couldn't afford their bills, Dad would often accept an Afghan blanket or other homemade treasure as payment.

The community was friendly and family-oriented, and Dad had chosen to settle there because it reminded him of his village back home. In our tiny Michigan town, a very small percentage of people ever moved away, only a third or so went on to college, and many married young. For the most part, it was an idyllic place to grow up.

We were big fish in a tiny pond, always in the spotlight. Everybody in the town knew who we were because of my dad's status as a doctor, and my dad knew everyone and everything going on because more than half the town were his patients. If a boy liked me, Dad always got the scoop before I did. "I heard from his mom that so-and-so has a crush on you. You better not even think about it!"

On the flip side, it seemed like there was a giant pressure placed on me to be well-behaved and succeed in school. I felt like I had to keep "earning my place" in the rags-to-riches story we'd landed in. The message I got from Mom was, *You better get good grades. You better act right. You better not mess this up.*

It also didn't help that Dad wasn't very verbose about his love for us at the time (he's since softened and frequently tells us he loves us). His love language was gifts—like Guess jeans or whatever clothing or shoes were popular at the time—but those were always given in response to achievements, like another straight A report card or academic award. The way I interpreted that was his approval solely depended on my accomplishments.

I also struggled watching as Dad's kids were allowed to live a very "American" lifestyle, like being able to date in high school, while my mom and dad were much stricter with me and my sister. They had a completely different set of rules for my half-Caucasian, Christian-raised stepsiblings than for us. I kept thinking, *Hey, wait, that's not fair!* Little did I know that one day I'd have three girls of my own and find myself having to set different rules for them based on their specific needs and circumstances. Life comes back to bite you that way sometimes.

Okay, confession time: There was one other big challenge I faced, both then and now. Wherever we went, we were the ones who didn't make sense. We were complete outliers within the greater Bangladeshi community—that we had to drive for hours to be with now—due to the multiple divorces, poverty, nontraditional foods and holidays, and mixed-race stepsiblings. Within our own town (and even a 50-mile radius of it), we were the only Brown and/or Muslim people. We didn't fit in at any mosque—not that there was one within easy driving distance at the time anyway—because our understanding of religion was less formally derived, coming only from what Mom had taught us. My friends in town didn't know any better, so they always assumed having darker skin meant I was Jamaican or African.

All this left me with a deep longing to find my true and rightful place in the world—but if that even existed, I certainly didn't know where it was.

Personal insight: My mother did not want to ask my uncle and aunt for additional help for childcare. My sister and I ended up being alone and in some unsafe situations. I can empathize with what my mother was feeling. She didn't want to be a burden. She wanted to do it on her own. I feel bad asking for help without me being able to reciprocate. I realize now there's no prize for carrying the most weight when someone is there, offering, and able to carry that weight *with* you.

Universal takeaway: The desire to prove something to yourself and others can come at a cost. There is strength in being able to accept help.

Chapter 2

Send Me on My Way

As my dad was one of two physicians in the area, he was on call 50% of the time. Likely for this reason, none of my stepsiblings had any interest in following in his footsteps. They hated having to break plans or drive in separate cars because his pager was always blowing up, and they equated that kind of lifestyle with the profession. Besides, they'd already defined their own passions in life, and medicine wasn't it. My stepbrothers had decided to go into engineering and my stepsister wanted to be a teacher. (As soon as Dad found that last one out, he started a fund for her because he thought, *Oh no! Teachers don't make any money!* Dad has always been concerned about the financial stability of all his children.)

Still, it was made clear that *someone* was going to have to take over Dad's practice one day, which left my sister and me as the only viable candidates. My sister started "acting out"—what other families might consider pretty normal experimentation, like sneaking out to meet boys and drinking alcohol. However, in our family, this was considered outrageous behavior. Therefore, she was ruled out as an heir to Dad's doctor throne. She was grounded for what seemed like an eternity and labeled the rebel, which meant the responsibility of taking over Dad's practice fell squarely on my shoulders.

I was the youngest and last child; if I didn't do it, who would? No one. I knew I had the ability, and it was my familial obligation. I *owed* it to Dad.

Besides, he'd been telling me for as long as I could remember, "Tasha, you're going to an Ivy League school to be a doctor someday." I vividly remember getting a Yale sweatshirt for Christmas in second grade, so it's no wonder I always assumed time in New Haven would be in my future, as well as a career in medicine. It wasn't so much an option as an edict.

I went to math and science camp from middle school on. Every summer, I'd head to a local college, where I'd stay in the dorms and learn about molecular biology or something equally as intellectually challenging. I took independent study math to climb the academic ladder more quickly. Throughout high school, I regularly pulled all-nighters to keep up with my grades and sports. Since there were no AP classes offered in my town, I attended the Math and Science Center at a local college as one of two students chosen to attend from my high school class. Each day, I took a big brown van to Andrews University in Berrien Springs, Michigan, to be with a bunch of other academically talented kids and take college-level classes from full-fledged college professors.

I missed out on a good portion of my high school experience with my friends because I was riding that van, but I was sure my sacrifice would be worth it someday when I achieved the ultimate prize: becoming a doctor. At the time, I often thought, *my biological father didn't want me, so I want to do everything I can to make Dad happy.* This was going to make him *very* happy.

And quite honestly, I thought being a doctor was going to make me very happy, too—as long as I didn't have to be a surgeon or have a surgeon's lifestyle. My still-secret small act of rebellion was that I was going to choose a specialty with a better schedule, because if there was one other thing I knew for sure about my future, it was that I was going to be a mom. I figured I'd probably get married someday—hopefully to a teacher who had summers off or a guy who wanted to stay at home with the kids full-time so I could focus on my practice—but I couldn't really envision him in any concrete way. But I knew I wanted kids.

As an undergrad, I pursued a biopsychology major at the University of Michigan in Ann Arbor (New Haven turned out to not be an option, much to my dad's chagrin). There, I found myself a tiny little fish in a big brainy pond. For the first time in my life, I did *not* stand out for my intellect. I felt completely mediocre in every way.

Still, it was fantastic on so many levels: no one cared what my last name was or expected anything from me because of it, no one knew me based on the fact that my dad was the town physician, and my lectures sometimes had as many as 650 people in them—over 500 more than my high school's graduating class. What a different experience!

I was now also one of many people of color and exposed to diverse populations and ideas I hadn't encountered before. Gender, race, culture, religion, sexuality, politics—everything I'd never talked about with my family or even friends back home was open for discussion here. I learned a lot, made a core group of friends I'm still close with today, and took on leadership roles, like being a resident advisor.

Interestingly, though, being in an atmosphere where many other people shared my South Asian heritage didn't help solve my "one of these things is not like the others" issue. In fact, I'd say it made my feeling of not fitting in worse. I became self-conscious, thinking, *They know so much more about our culture than I do! I can't relate to them, and they can't possibly relate to me.* I was so embarrassed by and ashamed of my lack of knowledge that I purposely chose not to join the groups that matched my identity during college or even try to connect with people who had similar identities. I know now that no one was judging me, but at the time, I really struggled with finding my place within my community of heritage.

Honestly, I still struggle with it. Sometimes patients will ask where my family is from and when I tell them, they'll invite us to a Bangladeshi or Indian community party. I always politely nod but never actually go—partly because of Soraya's special needs, but also because I continue to have a hard time figuring out where I fit in. I am very open about this with my friends and always ask for their forgiveness and grace. I'm still a work in progress, just like the rest of us.

Throughout much of college, I dated a guy who was the son of one of Dad's best friends, another Bangladeshi doctor who lived within driving distance. My family was happy about this, and because he was a Muslim, it made it easy for me to stay semi-religious during college. Sure, we'd have a beer at a party or bar (against the rules of Islam), but we also fasted together during Ramadan. It wasn't praying five or six times a day like my mom, but it was enough. Coincidentally, my sister was dating his brother at the time, and the joke was always that we'd marry them, and our families would become in-laws. Everyone *loved* this idea.

I already had an inkling that this wasn't the guy I was going to marry. I knew this well before meeting Mama Mary. She was a tarot expert my high school friend hired to do readings at her bachelorette party. She has since become a dear friend and has seen me through every phase of life. She definitely confirmed what I already knew about the future of my relationship. "This guy you're dating has no direction. If you put a suitcase in his hands, he would go wherever you went. He's like a lost puppy."

She nailed it. He was a nice guy, but whenever I asked about his goals for the future, he'd say, "Oh, I'll just follow you to med school." As much as my plan was to marry someone who would support my career as well as stay home with the kids, I also wanted that person to have a passion for *something* in life. This guy didn't seem to be passionate about anything—not even me. I think he was comfortable in our relationship, but that was about the extent of it.

12

Keep Your Head Up

Clearly, it wasn't meant to be. We broke up, but our dads remained steadfast in their friendship. There wasn't any animosity; it just wasn't a long-term fit for either of us. Done. Moving on.

While I was at Michigan, I went on a service trip dubbed Alternative Spring Break with my friend Soraya. She's half Persian, half Filipino, speaks several languages, and is brilliant in every way. I love her so dearly that I named my daughter after her.

That year, the trip was to Chicago. One day while we were working in a food pantry serving people with HIV/AIDS, I was talking with another student who told me she was applying to osteopathic medical schools. Although there were undoubtedly doctors of osteopathy in rural Michigan, I didn't know of any—or even what the differences between a DO (Doctor of Osteopathy) and an MD were—at the time. She explained that osteopathy took a more holistic approach to medicine, considering a patient's body, mind, and spirit rather than only the presenting symptoms.

My curiosity was piqued. I'd always been fascinated by how our biology affects our psychology, hence my major in biopsychology. I'd recently gone for a few counseling sessions at the student health center—I had a vague awareness that therapy would benefit me— and thought it was helpful. A holistic approach to medicine had a big appeal to me.

But then she added the kicker: "Most DOs are dedicated to working with underserved populations."

In that moment, it was like a lightning bolt struck me. Already, my plan was to move back to my hometown and take over my dad's practice after med school—and his practice was in a place that was underserved. The whole conversation felt like fate.

"YES!" I exclaimed. "That's exactly what I want to do and how I want to practice medicine!"

She leaned in closer and lowered her voice. "Some people also do it because it's a lot easier to get into school."

13

Send Me on My Way

If she thought that little truth bomb was going to turn me off, well, nope. It was just another giant draw. I'm not a good test taker, and I had my fears about not being able to get into an MD or an allopathic school anyway. By contrast, DO schools stressed well-roundedness in applicants, and I'd done all kinds of community service and knew I had a good bedside manner.

"Sweet! Easier to get into is great with me. Why would I stress myself out about trying to get the perfect MCAT score if I don't have to?"

The more I researched, the more the philosophy of the osteopathic world resonated with me. I loved how if a patient presented with, say, shoulder pain, DOs would look deeper to find out what was causing it (ergonomics, biomechanics, psychological and life stressors) and work to help rectify those issues rather than simply writing a prescription and sending them on their merry way. Being committed to the underserved was something already instilled in me by way of growing up in a rural town, and providing primary care in places where it was needed most fit my goals exactly.

Back when I was applying to med school, MDs were considered more research- and science-oriented while DOs were considered more holistic clinicians. Over time those definitions have evolved, and I don't think the differentiation between the two is as strong as it once was. Today, I feel like DOs are trying to establish themselves as more scientific while MDs are concerned with being more well-rounded, but at that time, they felt like entirely different approaches to medicine.

Becoming a DO was absolutely what I wanted to do with my life. It felt like I'd be staking a claim to my own identity, as opposed to becoming an MD simply because my family expected me to or because that's the stereotype expectation for a second-generation child.

I wanted to break that mold. I wanted to be different. I wanted to be *me*. Instead of being an MD surgeon like my dad, I'd become a hugging, loving, holistic, underserved-population-serving DO.

At first, I tiptoed lightly around the subject with him. "Do you know about osteopathic medicine, Dad?"

"Of course," he replied flatly. "In the 1960s, they all had to turn in their licenses and pay a fee to be recognized as physicians."

My stomach dropped. This was not going to be an easy sell. I ventured on. "Oh. Well, I want to become one."

"Why don't you want to go to an MD school?" he asked, giving me an indiscernible stare.

"I like their holistic approach to medicine," I replied, my stomach doing a sad little flip. "It's a different way of looking at people."

To be fair, I don't think Dad was against osteopaths—I just think he knew that there was a stigma. He thought it would be a harder road for me, and I don't think he was wrong about that. Still, I took his lack of enthusiasm very personally at the time and didn't feel supported in my decision.

I cared, but not enough to back down. If I was going to become a doctor, I was going to be the doctor *I* wanted to be.

Personal insight: I was so focused on becoming a doctor that I missed opportunities for joy. Taking the toughest courses, pulling all-nighters, and obsessing over where I would get into medical school meant missing out on simply being a teenager.

Universal takeaway: A career is not an identity. A career is a goal. Achieving a goal doesn't always equate to happiness. Don't forget to find happiness in your pursuit of goals.

Chapter 3

Perfect

There was never a time in my life when it would have been okay for me *not* to pick medicine as a career path. For as far back as I can remember, my parents' favorite joke was "We'll let you choose your husband as long as you become a doctor." It was always said with a laugh, but we all knew they were being dead serious (and becoming a doctor sounded way better to me than having an arranged marriage).

Yet even though I was firmly guided to this destination, I'm happy with where I ended up. I absolutely love my job. I've been lucky to develop deep, long-term relationships with the families in my practice, and it has been such a privilege to watch so many beautiful babies grow into feisty toddlers, curious school-aged children, passionate teens, and successful young adults. That's the natural progression of things, though the universe sometimes has other ideas—the shock, disappointment, and pain of which I now know all too well. The only consolation that comes from being intimately acquainted with the different path medically complex kids and their parents have to take is knowing my experience makes me a far more empathetic and well-informed doctor than I otherwise would have been.

Over the years, I've thought a lot about whether medicine would have been my chosen profession without all the added parental pressure. The answer I keep returning to is yes, though perhaps in a different capacity. One intriguing career I've encountered along this journey is genetic counseling. Geneticists have to get so personal, so fast, with their clients. At first the questioning seems incredibly intrusive—*What would you do if your child died? If you found out you carried a certain chromosome, would you have other children?*—but I've since come to understand how needed the service they provide is. Because it combines ethics, science, psychology, and the human condition—all areas I'm fascinated with—I could totally see myself doing that kind of work.

Back then, though, I didn't know anything about genetics or even pediatrics—Dad had always been my physician because my town didn't have a pediatrician—so I was fully on board with the plan to become a family practitioner and then join my dad's practice. Everything about it felt right: I knew I wanted to settle down somewhere close to my parents. I knew our tight-knit community would allow me to create long-lasting bonds with patients. And I also knew it would be an exceedingly smart financial move since Dad already had a booming practice and an office with our name on it in town. I'd be able to just walk in and keep it all going.

Honestly, the only thing I wasn't quite as certain about was where I was going to live post-graduation. I had this idea that the "big city"—South Bend—might be a good fit. It had all the amenities I was looking for, including a mall and a movie theater. And at just 26 miles away from my hometown, Dowagiac, the distance would enable me to commute back and forth to the office relatively easily.

But while living in South Bend instead of Dowagiac was something my parents would have happily accepted, me going to DO school instead of an MD one was an entirely different story. Although my mom didn't really understand the nuances of the two degrees, Dad worried I was setting myself up for undue hardship and started a subtle (and sometimes not-so-subtle) campaign for me to go the more traditional route. His negative reaction only compounded the giant pressure I was already putting on myself to succeed. Now beyond just being the Chosen One responsible for taking over my father's medical practice, it also felt like I needed to prove I was becoming a "real" doctor.

Still, when the time came, I stuck to my guns and applied only to DO schools. After evaluating all my acceptances, I chose a college in Arizona, despite the fact that it was private, and the tuition would put me into debt. One big factor in my decision was that my cousins—the children of the kind uncle, now deceased, we'd lived with so many years earlier—were in the area, and I was hoping to use proximity as an opportunity to reconnect. I'd always felt a kinship to them because we were raised together for a time, and being close to family was important to me. Even more so, though, was the fact that I was so positive I'd be back practicing medicine in my small hometown after graduating, I figured it would be a great time to spread my wings and live somewhere entirely different than where I'd grown up.

Things didn't go quite the way I planned, another big theme in my life (and everyone's, I suppose). My experience at Michigan had been so positive that I was convinced graduate school would be more of the same. It definitely wasn't. From day one, the academics in med school were harder than I expected. There weren't social events every night or friends to go to parties and bars with on the weekends. Many students were older and had more life and career experience than I did, not that it mattered anyhow since all we did was study. Having little to no social life, not to mention being so far from my parents and friends, left me feeling terribly isolated despite getting together with my cousins regularly.

It also didn't help that I was now in a long-distance relationship with a guy who happened to be Indian and Hindu. The message I'd always gotten from Mom and Dad was *you don't have to marry a Muslim, just make sure you're with someone who believes in God.*

19

Perfect

Unfortunately, there are long-standing cultural differences between Muslims and Hindus in South Asia that can make this pairing particularly difficult to navigate, so it was yet another choice my parents were less than thrilled about.

And then there was the fact that this boyfriend, who was now attending med school in Ohio, started escalating what had seemed to be a minor jealous streak once I got to Arizona. He'd call and demand to know what I was wearing, whom I was with, and whom I'd talked to that day. We'd danced around the idea of marriage prior to my heading off to school, but if this behavior was any indication of what our long-term life together was going to be like, it wouldn't be pretty. I started to wonder if this was what my mom had gone through with my biological father. I also wondered how I'd gotten myself into this situation—and how I was going to get myself out of it.

I tried breaking up with him countless times. In response, he would fly from Ohio to Arizona and show up at my doorstep unannounced, either begging me to stay or berating me for trying to end things. His behavior hit me as totally off, like something dangerous and potentially violent was always bubbling beneath the surface. I started living in fear of his unexpected visits. It felt like I was being stalked, and my friends swooped in to shield me.

After too many trips on this dysfunctional merry-go-round, the breakup finally stuck. While I anticipated feeling relief, my terror only increased. Knowing I'd considered marrying someone who'd acted so frighteningly erratic and treated me so poorly threw me for a total loop. How could I trust my judgment about anyone—or anything, really—anymore?

The turmoil in my personal life ended up spilling over into my academic life, and I failed my all-important first year anatomy class as a result. There was no opportunity for a summer makeup. That meant I'd have to take the class again in the fall with a whole new

Keep Your Head Up

cohort of students if I wanted to continue down the path of becoming a doctor. It seemed like an overwhelmingly shameful option, but I also didn't know what else to do. My whole life had been built on the assumption that I'd go into medicine. Who would I be without that identity? I didn't know, and I sure as hell didn't want to find out.

My many real and even more imagined failures dragged me down into depths I previously hadn't known existed. I'd had other hard times in high school—moments I felt the pressure of expectations so acutely I'd leaned into some unhealthy but effective coping mechanisms—but now I'd sunk far below what my old bad habits could assuage.

I found myself drowning in a relentless abyss: dark, black, foreboding. Everything felt slow and heavy, like I was on the ocean floor and couldn't break through to the surface no matter how hard I tried. Recognizing I needed help managing my mental health, I went to see the school therapist. Given the severity of my symptoms, the school recommended I consult with a psychiatrist. Although I was reluctant to do so, I felt like I had no choice since the request came directly from the dean.

Maybe I wasn't describing my situation as well as I could have or maybe we simply weren't a match, but either way I felt misunderstood by the doctor almost immediately. I was put on several medications that didn't agree with my chemistry, leaving me more adrift than ever. Things quickly went from dark to nihilistic.

I wanted to quit trying so hard all the time. I wanted to quit school. To be perfectly honest, I wanted to quit life.

Two dear friends, Lindsay and Cher, became my safety net to ensure I didn't act on my bleakest thoughts. Whenever I was worried that I might not be able to hang on any longer, I stayed overnight with them. They bathed me in love and light, which was disguised as bingeing our favorite shows and late-night talk sessions.

21

Perfect

After a while, a new plan began to form in my head: I'd go home and become a cashier at McDonald's. While I'm sure fast-food work has its fair share of pressures, at the time it sounded like a nice, low-stress job where I'd be able to shut off the nagging voice that kept telling me I wasn't *enough*—smart, motivated, talented, whatever—and never would be. I literally made my mom promise she'd still accept me if I quit school.

"Yes, Tasha," she told me. "I'd still accept you, and guess what? I'd still love you, too."

I remained unconvinced. I truly believed failing one class and being such a poor judge of my ex-boyfriend's character meant I was failing at life. I was certain my dad was mad at me for what, in my view, was a colossal, undoable academic blunder and I thought, *he'll never approve of me now*. As I remember it, he stopped talking to me during that time (or maybe I stopped talking to him, or maybe we stopped talking to each other). In retrospect, I think he may just have been worried about me and not verbalizing it, but however things really went down, I'd never felt more alone or untethered as when I realized I no longer fit the perfect child image I'd always tried to portray.

I wish I could have told myself back then *of course you can go work at McDonald's—you can do whatever you want. If medicine is still your passion, great, go do that class over again. If not, try something else. It's not the end of the world to change your mind, course, or direction in life. In fact, sometimes it's a gift.*

But I didn't have that kind of insight or life experience just yet, so I did the next best thing: I temporarily moved to New York City to live with my brilliant, sophisticated friend Soraya. She knew I was floundering around in a sea of depression and confusion. She also knew the last thing I wanted to do that summer was either be stuck in the Arizona heat overthinking my inadequacies or go back home under a cloud of disgrace only to be greeted with the silent treatment.

Oh, how right she was. Just as Soraya's encouragement to join her on the alternative spring break trip had been the key to unlocking my path to becoming a DO, the reprieve she offered me now turned out to be both life-affirming and life-changing. That invitation to get me out of my misery and into New York City became the key to unlocking my identity and potential.

I decided to spend that summer writing a book, so every morning I'd head off to a cool little neighborhood coffee shop to document my life and sift through the rubble of what it had become. My main goal was to find purpose in my pain and hope in my hardships, and when I did, I was damn sure going to use what I'd learned to help others. *Doctor, writer, what's the difference*, I thought. *I'll be of service to the world no matter what.*

Maybe it was the nonstop creative energy of the City that Never Sleeps seeping into my bones, or maybe the "real me" finally got sick of being trapped inside the box I'd been wrapped up in my whole life—*Tasha, you're going to be a doctor, put on your Yale sweatshirt, you will not mess this up, you will get straight As, fit in, get along, excel, succeed*—but I soon stepped into my power in ways I'd never been able to before. I stopped caring so much about what others thought or expected of me and instead went in the direction of what excited me. What piqued my curiosity. What I could fully call my own.

I pierced my nose. Wrote the truth. Spoke the truth. Cranked up the tunes. Just as Green Day, the Smashing Pumpkins, and Rage Against the Machine had been a salve for my high school heartaches, the Postal Service and Death Cab for Cutie were now along for the self-discovery ride with me.

I dove deeper into the alternative healing methods I'd already been exploring with some uber-talented fellow classmates back at school: Reiki, cranial-sacral therapy, energy work. I had more tarot readings from Mama Mary. Clearly the traditional path wasn't working for me, so I figured, why not try a different way? While my nontraditional seeking may have been partially fueled by desperation, I was happy to find comfort, relief, and a sense of calm on the other side of it.

I suppose my "becoming" that summer could have been seen by others—my parents, ill-fitting ex-boyfriends, and maybe even a culture of origin—as an act of rebellion. A strange kind of pity party or toddler-esque tantrum I was throwing myself in response to the disappointing events of the past year. But if that was the impression people had, they were dead wrong. It was about coming home to myself—my *true* self, and not who everyone else thought I should be.

The evolving "new" me reminded me a lot of my maternal grandmother, who had sadly recently passed. As a result of all those long days riding in that ugly brown van to do college coursework while I was still in high school, I'd finished up my undergrad requirements a semester early. I used the extra time to do research on women's reproductive health in Bangladesh, living with my Nani while I was there. During that trip, I learned—to my great surprise and delight—that she'd been taught to hunt, fish, and ride horses as a child, enjoying a somewhat feral existence. It was the polar opposite of how girls in our culture are usually raised, especially during that time frame. But her father—my great-grandfather—had lost his first wife to childbirth as well as three sons to febrile illness, and he'd decided to raise my grandmother as a "replacement son" in response to his overwhelming grief. She was more than happy to oblige and go against the conventions of society, and now I was, too.

By the end of my time in New York, I felt like I'd resurfaced and rejoined the world. And while I was nowhere close to finishing my book, I now had a better plan for moving forward with my life than quitting on everything I'd ever wanted: I'd go back to school, start over fresh, and I'd become an even better DO than I would have if this whole debacle hadn't happened—because now I had personal experience dealing with mental health struggles and alternative healing modalities that I'd be able to reference when helping my future patients.

My transformation from the perfect child who did everything everyone always expected of her to a fearless fighter who let her inner guidance rule the roost was complete. It was time for a do-over.

Personal insight: Failing anatomy class and taking an extra year in medical school felt like the end of the world. Without feeling that type and depth of failure, I would never have broken the pattern of trying to plan *everything*. Learning this helped prepare me for my future.

Universal takeaway: It's not the end of the world to change your mind, course, direction in life, or to fail. In fact, sometimes it's a gift. Sometimes failing enables us a do-over that also helps us evolve into a better version of ourselves.

Chapter 4

Take the Power Back

Despite my newfound confidence, I headed back to Arizona as a "second year first year" student with more than a little trepidation. It was a bummer that I was now in a different class than the people I'd bonded with the year before, especially Cher and Lindsay, the two dear friends who'd essentially saved my life when I was mired in darkness. It was awkward meeting my new cohort and having to explain why I wasn't in *all* their classes—I'd only failed anatomy, so there was no need to retake the other subjects that were regular first-year requirements. And I felt stuck between the two groups, forever worrying what both were thinking of me. Was it something like *what a loser, she couldn't hack it, she's not smart enough to do this, poor thing*? I hoped not but assumed so.

I gathered up all the strength and courage my friend Soraya had helped me build over the summer and decided *Okay, I already don't fit in, so I'm just going to carve my own path*. As it turns out, having all that extra time in my schedule was a blessing in disguise. I started substitute teaching and volunteering for Big Brothers Big Sisters, allowing me to be of service to the community—one of my deepest-held core values. If I'd been on the regular first-year schedule, there wouldn't have been any room for anything but studying. As another added and unexpected bonus, having a more balanced life made me realize how much more focused, productive, and efficient I can be when I'm not depressed.

As I was working on finding my footing with both sets of classmates, I was also actively avoiding dating. I wasn't ready to trust myself and my discernment in that area again quite yet. Doing well in school and continuing to focus on my personal growth were my main goals for the year.

Bridget, a fellow student and cranial sacral goddess, had other ideas for me. In DO school, upperclassmen are eligible for special fellowships if they're really good at what they do, and Bridget was as good as it gets. This magical, warm, authentic creature was now serving as a teaching assistant in one of my classes, and she had a way of drawing people to her naturally. We became fast friends despite her status as a fourth year and mine as a "second year first year."

Bridget approached me one day after class with a seemingly innocent question. "Are you dating anyone?"

"Nope, no men this year," I told her. "I'm concentrating all my efforts on school."

"But I have the perfect person for you!" she exclaimed. "His name is Safi and he's a fourth year."

"Not interested. Not doing it."

"He's at the Naval Hospital right now," she pressed on. "Honestly, I think you guys are a perfect match."

In the final year of med school, students explore different rotations at a variety of hospitals, using them as a kind of tryout for residency placements. According to Bridget, this guy was currently in Virginia. Already he was geographically undesirable—strike one against him. And in the military? Strike two. I was going back to my hometown to take over my dad's practice after my own residency, not traipsing around the world at the whim of some dude and his deployments.

Besides, whats-his-face sounded vaguely like it could be a South Asian name, quite possibly Indian—and that was strike three, big-time. After I finally managed to extract myself from that last awful relationship, I promised myself I'd never date anyone Indian again. Was it unfair to condemn an entire country of men just because of one bad boyfriend? Yes, but I still had post-traumatic stress disorder from his treatment of me and the seemingly endless depressive episode that followed. I wasn't taking any chances.

I was even giving this guy a strike four, and it was a biggie: I got the feeling—maybe also unfair—that Bridget was only thinking he and I would be cute together because we were both Brown. It was just another box I didn't want to stay inside of anymore. After exclusively being in relationships with guys from a similar background, I thought it was about time for some equal opportunity dating.

Hanging out with someone from a different culture and religion sounded like a fantastic idea for whenever I was ready to get back out there. Which wasn't yet, that's for sure. Everything I was putting out in the universe was the exact opposite of what Bridget was offering me, so it was going to have to be a "thanks, but no thanks" from me.

Fortunately, she let it go. Unfortunately, it was only for the moment. Turns out, she was just waiting for another opportunity to get me and this guy together.

The next week, Bridget invited me to have lunch with her after class. I happily obliged. On the way there, she casually mentioned that her husband, Travis, a fellow student, would be joining us. No problem, I told her. I liked him and was perfectly content to be the third wheel.

Until I found out there was a fourth wheel. That is, Safi.

I was wearing sweatpants, and he walked up to our table looking like he was going to the hottest club in Miami. My hair was swept up into a messy bun, and his hair was gelled to perfection. He announced he was from Iowa. *Another Midwestern guy?* I thought. *Nope. This is not happening.*

The only bright spot during lunch was when Safi mentioned he had premium seats, courtesy of one of his mentors, to a Phoenix

Suns game that weekend and asked us all to go. I'd never seen the team play and decided it was a totally safe invitation since it was a group outing. Something fun and social to do in a place where I hardly ever got to do social things. I said yes.

I felt decent about my decision for about 10 minutes. By the time I got back to my apartment, though, I was practically hyperventilating. Cher was the lucky beneficiary of my freak-out.

"What am I doing? I said no men this year. I don't like this guy. In fact, I think I might even hate him!"

"Go anyhow," she advised me. "It'll be fun."

"I just hope it's not a setup," I snapped, and I headed to my room with the intention of studying but ending up mostly fuming about the situation instead.

The night before the game, Bridget texted me—surprise, surprise—to let me know she and Travis wouldn't be able to go after all. She had some lame excuse that no one in their right mind would believe. My suspicions about this being a date in disguise were confirmed.

If you're not going, I'm not going, I texted back quickly.

Maybe you guys can just be friends, she replied. *Who knows? Safi might turn out to be someone you can hang out with casually.*

I already have enough friends, I replied, done with the conversation.

After what can only be described as begging on Bridget's part, I finally agreed to go. But just because I'd given in to her didn't mean I had to be nice about it. This Safi guy was going to get the bare minimum from me, so he knew without a doubt I wasn't interested.

My irritation grew when Safi announced he'd be picking me up a full two hours before the game started. What kind of guy picks you up at 4:30 for a date? My apartment was only 15 miles from the arena! *Watch this be the longest date of my life*, I thought. I concocted a getaway plan with Cher in case I couldn't stand being

30

Keep Your Head Up

with him a second longer or on the off chance he turned out to be a true psychopath.

Safi picked me up early as promised, once again nauseatingly perfect in his presentation. I hadn't even bothered changing out of the ratty old jeans I'd worn to class that day, and he was dressed up like an Armani ad. His car was spotless. Worst of all, he was wearing cologne. He even *smelled* like he thought he was on a date, which hit me as beyond presumptuous.

I went from mildly unwilling into total brat mode, just barely deigning to answer the multitude of questions he lobbed at me on the ride there. Whenever he stopped talking, the silence became deafening. We pulled into the pregame restaurant he'd chosen for its proximity to the stadium to the sound of me sighing heavily.

"Do you have any dietary restrictions?" he asked as we perused our menus. If nothing else, I was impressed by his sheer determination and resilience. I was giving him exactly zero to go on, yet he just kept plowing ahead.

"I don't eat pork," I replied.

"Oh, I don't mess with swine, either," he quipped.

"Wait, are you Muslim?"

Safi nodded.

"And are you . . . Persian?" I guessed, taking a stab in the dark. I'd been wondering about the answer to this one since we'd met, so I figured I might as well come right out and ask him. Persian, Turkish, Algerian, Egyptian, Lebanese—anything but Indian—was the correct answer.

"No, I'm Indian," he replied.

And that was that. Not that I'd ever particularly thought there was a chance we'd become a couple, but now I knew without the slightest doubt. The relationship potential here was dead on arrival.

A little girl started playing a video game within eyeshot of our table. I've always been automatically drawn to children, so I turned

31

Take the Power Back

my attention away from Safi and toward her. When her time on the machine ran out, Safi got up and gave her a dollar so she'd be able to try her hand at a few more games.

My mood quickly morphed from annoyance back to all-out disgust. *What a low blow! He probably doesn't even like kids—he's just showing off*, I thought. In my mind, it was all an act designed to impress me (the truth is Safi absolutely adores children, but I didn't know that at the time). I thought about faking a headache just so I could get out of the rest of this night, but I controlled the unkind urge.

When we got to the arena, all that pent-up irritation, annoyance, and disgust started to dissipate again. By now it was apparent Safi wasn't a psychopath, so I knew I was safe. There was nothing *so* hideous about him that I couldn't stand being with him any longer, so I wouldn't need to implement the escape plan I'd hatched with my friends before I left. And since this was going nowhere, I had nothing to lose. I decided to just relax and have fun.

The game got underway, and I gradually let my guard down. When Safi asked about my childhood, I was open with him about my biological dad, the divorce, and feeling inadequate about my knowledge of my religion and culture because of where and how I was raised. I think part of me wanted to show him I didn't fit in the box I assumed he thought I did, and another part felt a huge kind of relief being able to talk about topics that weren't open for discussion within my family and that I'd always lived in fear of uttering a peep about to anyone because it might ruin our sterling and all-important reputation in town.

Safi took it all in and responded with understanding and empathy. He seemed intrigued by what I was saying—my family's story, relationships, and challenges—but the thing that drew me most to him was his view of my personal struggles as amazing as opposed to *oh boy, you have a lot of baggage.* He felt like a really safe and open person to tell the unvarnished truth to.

And I wasn't the only one opening up, either. Safi confided in me that he'd moved to Arizona to date a white woman. His parents disapproved of her, refusing to give up hope that he'd agree to an arranged marriage like his brother had. Despite their wishes, he'd planned on proposing to this girlfriend—until he walked in on her cheating on him. This outwardly perfect guy apparently had more depth to him than I ever imagined and wasn't afraid to be authentic or vulnerable. His story even sounded eerily like my dad's!

We talked through the entire game, barely watching any of the action on the court. Our conversation seamlessly transitioned from joking and laughing to dead serious and back again. *Hey, look at me, I'm actually having fun*, I thought. *Cher was right.*

By that point in the night, my feelings for Safi had shifted from "I hate you" to "I like you." Not I "like" like you, but in the "we can definitely be friends" kind of way, just as Bridget had suggested. I made a mental note to stop being so suspicious of my friends' motives and start trusting them more in the future. They seemed to know me even better than I knew myself sometimes, and they'd always had my back and best interests at heart.

Neither Safi nor I wanted the date to end after the game, so we headed to a bar for more conversation. We were chatting and telling jokes when an ad for the movie *Dodgeball* came on the TV. "I love that movie!" I exclaimed. Safi said he did, too, so we spontaneously decided to go rent it (yes, this was in the good old days when there was a Blockbuster on practically every corner).

Back at my apartment, we popped in the DVD and started watching the movie. I snuck a glance over at Safi and thought, *well, maybe I could kiss him just for fun.* A few scenes later, I decided, *yeah, I can definitely kiss him.* I made the first move, we shared a sweet kiss, and then the date was over. It was ultimately an enjoyable night but whether I saw him again or not didn't matter. Either way would be fine with me.

As I said goodbye and shut the door behind him, I suddenly remembered a dream I'd had a few weeks prior. In it, my deceased uncle—the one we'd lived with after bio dad dumped us off at his house, whose wife and kids I'd recently reconnected with in Arizona—was sitting in my apartment. He looked at me very seriously and said, "That last guy was not the one for you, the next guy is. He's such a good guy, he's who you need to marry." I'd chalked it up to the weirdness of the rapid eye movement cycle then, just like I was chalking this non-date date up to nothing more than a fun night now. In no way, shape, or form did I believe that Safi was my future husband. (Apparently, though, after he left my apartment, Safi went home and told his roommate, "I just met my wife!" so he and my dead uncle were totally on the same wavelength.)

When people ask us today, *Was it love at first sight?* I always have to laugh. No, it wasn't like that at all. It was a roller coaster of emotions that took us time to recognize and understand.

But were we meant to be? Yes, although there were some big twists and turns before we were both able to come to that conclusion. Little did we know then that those twists and turns would just keep on coming even after we realized we were in this thing together for the long haul.

Especially after.

Personal insight: I went on a date I never wanted to go on and I went with someone I never thought could be a good fit for me.

Universal takeaway: Sometimes we may not know what or whom we need in our lives until we actually meet them and get to know them.

Going into a date with little expectations can sometimes get you further than you think as you may be more yourself when you feel like you have nothing to lose!

Chapter 5

Nothing Better

The next day, Safi called and asked me to go see *Ocean's Eleven* with him. I was surprised to hear from him so soon and loved how he was flaunting "the rules." He didn't care that he was "supposed" to wait five days before contacting me again. It seemed I had a fellow rebel on my hands, which made me like him—but you know, not in the boyfriend kind of way—even more.

We had a good time at the movies, so I invited him to come over to my apartment afterwards. "Sure, but I'm not staying the night," he told me.

It was maybe five o'clock at the time. The sun was still out. I definitely hadn't been thinking about a sleepover. "No one invited you to," I shot back at him.

Our lighthearted conversation suddenly dried up, and neither of us could figure out what to say or do next. After an endlessly awkward silence, Safi looked at me super seriously and said, "I think we need to break up."

When Safi joined the navy in grad school as an officer, it wasn't a case of *I'm doing this to pay for my schooling and then get out as quickly as possible*. Coming off an idyllic semester abroad in Peru as an undergrad, he envisioned his life in the military as adventure-filled, nonstop excitement. He had great friends following the same path and could have easily made a career out of it. Not to mention, after the cheating girlfriend debacle, being tied down wasn't part of his plan for the foreseeable future anymore.

35

All of which is why, after telling his roommate he'd just met his future wife the night before, Safi started freaking out. He thought, *I'm about to match in my orthopedic residency, I'm in the military, and I could get deployed anywhere in the world, so this is no time to jump into a serious relationship. Tasha is either going to be my wife or we can't see each other at all.*

I think Safi was expecting me to burst into tears or express terrible disappointment that he was "breaking up" with me instead of what I actually did—which was start laughing so hard I could barely find the words to respond. "*You* break up with *me*? What are you talking about? We're not even going out!"

"What?" He seemed dumbfounded.

"First of all, you're not my boyfriend," I explained. "Second of all, I'm not your girlfriend. And third of all, we can't break up because we were never together in the first place."

Safi stared at his feet, the walls, the ceiling, anywhere but at me as a blush crept up his cheeks. I think he realized he'd just overreacted big-time. "I just don't want this to get in the way of me being a hand surgeon," he mumbled.

"Your career? What about my career? I'm in medical school, too, you know!" I was practically yelling now. "Nobody's getting in the way of *my* dreams after working so hard!"

After more ridiculous conversation along these same lines, we somehow agreed we were going to date, just not seriously. It was probably the fastest change of heart in history for both of us. I'd gone from "hating" this guy yesterday to yelling at him for thinking he could break up with me today, and he'd gone from thinking I was his future wife last night to needing to be talked out of leaving me at the altar less than twenty-four hours later.

At the time, I was having regular Sunday night dinners with my aunt in Arizona. That week, I mentioned to her that I'd gone on a date a few days before. She got all excited and patted the couch next to her. "Ooooh, come tell me about him."

I hadn't even finished sitting down before I started listing the many reasons she shouldn't become too attached to this guy. "He's Indian. He's in the military. He's Muslim. But he's definitely not the one for me. So don't worry, I'm not marrying him." It soon became an inside joke in the family. *Hey, I went out with that guy that I'm not marrying again!*

She believed me, of course. I even believed it myself. But Mama Mary had a different opinion. During our next reading she told me, "This new guy is the person you're going to marry."

"Nope, I don't see it," I said, shooing away her proclamation like a pesky fly. "I'm totally not interested in him like that."

"Just you wait," she told me.

Throughout all our mutual doubt, fretting, and angst, Safi and I kept right on seeing each other. Things progressed casually between us at first, then gradually took on a deeper and more serious tone. We were in San Diego helping a friend look for an apartment when I decided to make another first move—a much bigger one than back when I'd decided to kiss him on our first non-date date.

We were walking hand in hand down the sun-drenched beach when I blurted out, "I love you."

Silence. Silence. Silence. Then Safi said, "Look, I just matched for a civilian residency in Toledo. I think we need to put an end to this now. The logistics are just too complicated."

It was so on brand I couldn't help but smile despite how embarrassing it was to have just professed my love to a guy who was trying to get rid of me in response. "Dude, what is *wrong* with you? I'm not going to get in the way of your career and I'm not looking to get married. Can't we just see what happens?"

Another round of ridiculous conversation that sounded a lot like the first time he tried to break up with me ensued. Again, our hearts

37

Nothing Better

shifted. And in the end, we decided to try long distance and let the chips fall where they may. We'd both be busy, and either it would work out or it wouldn't.

The first two years of med school take place in the classroom, and the last two are spent doing rotations in the clinical setting to get experience in a variety of specialties. By this time, I was nearing the end of the pure classroom portion of my med school education and about to start my rotations. Attending a private DO college without a roster of strong affiliations meant I'd have to find hospitals to accept me rather than receiving placement assistance from the school. It was one of those things my dad had worried about when I'd chosen to go this route, and it required a lot of determination and hustle.

I was already using my Midwestern roots as a selling point. My pitch went something like this: *I'm from a small town in Michigan. I plan to practice medicine in an underserved, rural area in this part of the country when I graduate. Will you take me as a student?*

Hospitals must have liked what they heard, because I was able to schedule clinical rotations at all the best places in Chicago and Indiana. But despite wanting to be close to Safi, I couldn't quite make myself start cold-calling places in Ohio just yet. In planning my life—I was always trying to plan my life back then—that state had never once factored into my thinking.

"Why not just set up some things in Toledo?" Safi encouraged me. "Keep it open as an option."

I felt like there were just too many unknowns to do that. Safi now had a five-year orthopedic surgery residency to complete. He wanted to follow that up with a hand surgery fellowship, but he also knew there was a good chance he'd get deployed after the residency ended. In that case, the fellowship would have to wait until he returned from wherever the navy decided to ship him off to.

I started thinking long and hard about our relationship and what, if any, future we might have together. *Where do I see Safi in my life?*

38

Keep Your Head Up

Do I really want to put all my eggs in this one basket? Do I actually have any interest in going to Ohio—for a boyfriend no less? Maybe I should just do my own thing and see if it all lines up in the end.

Besides, I had my own commitment I'd made to the National Health Service Corps. In exchange for financial assistance with my med school tuition, I'd agreed to work as a doctor in an underserved, economically disadvantaged community for four years after I graduated residency. The NHSC only paid tuition if you went into primary care, which included family medicine, pediatrics, internal medicine, and ob/gyn. This just added to the challenge of us trying to be together in the same location as we navigated our schooling.

On and on I tried to envision my life with Safi and my life without him. Both paths seemed exceedingly complicated. In the end, I told him, "I'm only willing to change my life plan for someone I can see myself being with forever. So, if we're not on that path, I'll do my own thing and we can continue to just date." I truly wasn't giving him an ultimatum—I was just being totally transparent about my thinking.

Safi moved to Toledo that July. By October, he had—unbeknownst to me—asked for my parents' permission to propose. (I always joked that Toledo's dating scene was so bad he had no other options.) By December, we were engaged.

We dove directly into some deep and serious conversations about how we would balance the demands of our individual careers after that. We both agreed that while not everything could always be 50–50—sometimes it would be more about one person's job, and other times it would be the opposite person's turn—as long as it all evened out in the end, we could both get on board with that compromise. That decided, there was no doubt in my mind I'd follow Safi to Ohio.

My parents were again less than thrilled with this choice. I'd already done clinical rotations at the University of Michigan and

Cleveland Clinic, using my time there as a sort of audition for a potential residency. Now I was giving up the opportunity to be a resident in a prestigious program like those for a tiny, noncompetitive, under-the-radar one in Toledo. They just couldn't wrap their heads around it.

I understood their disappointment, but I also felt very strongly about Safi and me being together as much as we could, given the circumstances. I saw a future with my husband that included being separated by a military deployment at some point. While I had no choice in when or where that might be, I never wanted to look back and say, *I could have been with you during my residency, but I chose not to.*

Because we both come from very traditional families—Safi's even more so than mine—there was no way we were going to live together before we were married, so we timed our marriage to coincide with when I'd be moving to Toledo for most of my clinical rotations and after that my residency. This made our engagement extremely short by necessity—just a little over six months long.

We went ahead and scheduled the wedding for the following August.

Personal insight: I sacrificed moving *anywhere* and being in *any* residency program in order to be together. I have no regrets as Toledo was a gem of a program and I learned I could make the best of any educational program by giving it my all and being grateful for the opportunity.

Universal takeaway: Marriage takes compromise. You can't always both have what you want, even if both of you are in demanding careers.

Chapter 6

Father of Mine

In early July, I packed up my things, said goodbye to my classmates, and started driving home from Arizona. My bachelorette party and bridal shower were scheduled for that weekend in Grand Rapids. Friends and relatives had already begun flying in from around the country. I was beyond excited.

After the parties were over, the plan was to begin my first rotation of med school with Dad as my preceptor—a clinical instructor who oversees medical students or residents as they learn about different specialties—in rural medicine. My school had approved this unusual arrangement, and I was totally looking forward to being mentored by him. It was going to give us some good bonding time, not to mention provide me with a great glimpse into what my future medical practice would look like. Besides, I was getting married in a month. It was the perfect time to be close to home, not to mention the wedding venue.

I was halfway home to Michigan when my mom told me she was worried that my dad didn't seem to be bouncing back very quickly from the scheduled gallbladder surgery he'd had a few days earlier. My mom's not a clinician and recovery often takes longer than lay people expect it to. I wasn't too concerned.

When I saw for myself what was going on, though, my assessment of the situation changed quickly. I took one look at my dad and thought, *Oh boy, Mom was right. He doesn't look good.* His eyes were jaundiced. His belly was distended. His urine was really dark.

All I could think about was the pathology textbook I'd just studied with a graphic of Charcot's triad: fever, jaundice, and abdominal pain. It never meant anything good.

I called Safi and told him what was happening, ticking off the alarming symptoms. Even though neither one of us was a "real" doctor yet, we thought through all sorts of different scenarios using everything we'd learned in med school as the basis for our possible diagnoses. Safi's hypothesis was there might be a stone stuck somewhere and told me to keep an eye out for a high fever. I tucked his warning into the back of my mind and went to pick up my sister from the airport.

As soon as she hopped in the car, I relayed my concerns about Dad to her. I still wasn't envisioning anything terrible, but I also knew things weren't going as well as they should. She did her best to assure me everything was fine, but I just couldn't shake the feeling of impending doom.

We went to bed early that night, so we'd be well rested for the bachelorette party the next day. My mom woke us up from a dead sleep at two in the morning. "Your dad's completely out of it," she told us, panic rising in her voice. "He has a 103 degree fever and he's not making any sense."

We rushed him to the local hospital, where he also had admitting privileges. His colleagues there examined him carefully, trying to determine what was wrong. Although they couldn't figure out exactly what had happened or why, they soon discovered that Dad's bilirubin level was high. Bilirubin is a waste product that the body creates and typically passes through the liver, the bile ducts that attach to the liver, and is eventually excreted out of the body. Higher than usual levels of bilirubin may mean different types of liver or bile duct problems. Dad was hovering around an eight—and a normal reading is less than one. They advised us to go back to the hospital in Kalamazoo where he'd had the surgery to consult his doctor there.

We loaded Dad into an ambulance with my mom at his side while my sister and I followed in a separate car. Along the way, I scrambled to figure out plan B for my bachelorette party. I decided I would wait until the current crisis had passed and then proceed on with the festivities as planned. Kalamazoo was closer to Grand Rapids than home anyway, so this was just a little pit stop. *All the doctors need to do is remove the trapped stone and Dad will be on the road to recovery*, I thought. *Then we can all head off to the party.*

I had no doubt the surgeon who'd performed the operation would solve the problem quickly and efficiently, especially since he and my dad were *tight*. They'd been best friends since my dad started practicing in Michigan. Our families were so close, we'd always referred to him as our uncle.

He was already at the hospital when we showed up, looking incredibly upset. I took it as a sign of his love and concern for my dad's well-being. I started peppering him with questions, but he said he had no idea why Dad was having such a difficult and complicated recovery.

While we all waited and worried, another surgeon performed an emergency scope on my dad. At the time, we assumed the goal was to retract any stone that might have remained inside and repair any bleeds. We expected the procedure to be simple and effective, lead to a successful outcome, and result in a quick recovery.

It was none of those things. "I couldn't finish," the doctor soon reported back to us.

My heart started ricocheting around in my chest. "What do you mean, you couldn't finish?"

"I think his bile duct was cut during the operation," he explained matter-of-factly, as if this weren't completely shocking news on so many levels. "At this point, he needs reconstructive surgery, and it has to be done at a facility that does liver transplants in case one becomes necessary."

My mom went into a full-on panic attack, hyperventilating while rocking vigorously in the waiting room chair when she heard the news. I kept it all together on the outside, but I wasn't doing much better than her internally. How could this have happened, especially with a beloved "family member" doing the original routine surgery?

Even though Safi was spending his very first night on call at his brand-new residency, the serious and emergent nature of Dad's condition made me reach out to him. "Your two options are the University of Michigan or Henry Ford Hospital," he told me, deep concern seeping into his voice. "Hang in there. The surgeon will make arrangements for you."

In my head, I was like *Oh, please let it be Michigan, I know and love the area and especially that hospital.* Sadly, though, Michigan didn't have an opening. Henry Ford did. Off to Detroit we went.

But first, my sister and I stopped in to see Mama Mary, who lived nearby in Grand Rapids. We caught her just as she was finishing up doing readings for my bachelorette party guests. As always, she provided me guidance, comfort, and strength. Then I told my friends I had to stay with my dad because his condition was serious, and they should continue the bachelorette party minus the bachelorette. We were all in tears, most especially me.

My stepsiblings were already in town for my wedding shower, so they met us at the hospital in Detroit. Doctors soon determined Dad was suffering from sepsis—a serious and potentially life-threatening blood infection—because of the surgery. They started IV antibiotics while prepping him for another operation to find and fix whatever had gone wrong the first time. By that point, Dad was so out of it, he was muttering gibberish about his kidneys.

During the reconstructive surgery, the doctors at Henry Ford determined that not only had my dad's bile duct been cut during the botched procedure, but it had been fully severed. They did their best to repair the resulting liver damage but warned us Dad might never regain full function of the organ again. While the injury and its aftermath were terrible, the huge betrayal committed by my uncle was far worse.

As Dad was recovering from the second lifesaving surgery, he came to visit. When my dad saw his best friend turned betrayer, he started crying. It was almost more than I could bear.

"I know what you did," I said, seething with the white-hot intensity of a thousand suns.

"I don't know how I could have done anything differently," he replied, giving me a little shrug as if to say "eh, these things happen." "There was a lot of blood."

"So, you sent him home to die?" I hissed, grabbing him by the hand and dragging him to the door. I pointed to the exit. "You need to leave now, and don't you ever come back."

Dad spent the next 28 days in the hospital. During that time, he endured several life-threatening GI bleeds as well as a pulmonary embolism. Between the excellent care the doctors at Henry Ford gave him and Safi, me, and my sister—who dutifully flew back and forth from San Francisco where she lives—serving as his round-the-clock bedside advocates, we somehow managed to keep him alive and my mom sane throughout it all.

Dad got discharged at the end of July, a weaker, frailer, more infection-prone version of his former self. His diminished physical capacities were hard for us all to accept. To this day, he is prone to sudden bouts of fever followed by sepsis and frequent serious hospitalizations. Even before I had a special needs child, I always had a "go bag" in the trunk of my car in case of an emergency. It got put to good use then, as it still does now.

Still, there were a few positives that came out of the traumatic string of events. The first was that my dad was now more emotionally aware and expressive than he had been before his illness. This newfound softness in his demeanor was a bonus in my favor. The very first time he ever said *I love you* to me was when he was in the hospital. I was 25 years old at the time.

Another unexpected blessing was watching how Safi stepped up to the plate for us during my dad's health crisis. After working a 30-hour shift on the first day of his residency, Safi drove to Detroit to be with us—and he just kept right on coming after that. He made it his job to care for my dad, explain what was happening to my mom and siblings, and act as a liaison between us and the medical staff. I was beyond grateful he helped my father with the urinal, bedpan, and all the other things that would have been so awkward and embarrassing for me to do during that time.

His steadfast calm in the storm attitude was the key to helping us weather my dad's crisis—and many more trials yet to come.

Personal insight: My dad was so humbled by being ill. He saw how much he was loved and was finally able to verbalize his love for me. Seeing Safi care for my dad more than I would have ever expected made me love him even more.

Also when it comes to our family friend operating on my dad, there was too much that got in the way. I imagine those things added pressure, and ego.

Universal takeaway: Seeing someone at their worst can sometimes bring out the best within them. Watching how someone responds in times of crisis and need is an excellent indicator of how they will respond in those types of situations in the future. Last, don't let your best friend operate on you, and if you're a surgeon don't operate on your best friend.

Chapter 7

Follow You into the Dark

Instead of planning for our big day and basking in the festivities that led up to it, Safi and I spent the entire month before our wedding tending to my father. Of course, we wouldn't have had it any other way—family is of the utmost importance to both of us—but it certainly wasn't the excitement and anticipation most couples get to enjoy during that time. What we got instead, though, was worth far more than the lost opportunities: a deeper bond than I ever could have imagined possible. If I hadn't already known what an amazing partner Safi was before this, he'd now proven it beyond the shadow of a doubt.

We'd talked about possibly postponing our wedding many times during my dad's illness. I needed my father to be able to walk me down the aisle, and if he couldn't do that, it would just have to wait. Once Dad was safely recovering at home, though, we decided to go forward with the ceremony while shifting many of the details to accommodate his fragile health. By that point I was like, *I don't really care what this thing looks like anymore; let's just have an awesome party.*

Although we'd originally intended to get married in Chicago—about halfway between my hometown of Dowagiac, Michigan, and where Safi's family lives in Davenport, Iowa—we ended up choosing South Bend as our wedding location. It was less expensive and less complicated in terms of planning, not to mention closer to home.

Now that Dad was in no condition to travel very far, I was beyond grateful for the decision.

I knew I should've been ecstatic that everything was working out despite the difficult circumstances, but I was still grappling with the feeling that I didn't belong. This time, it was within the dynamics of Safi's family. I'd hoped his parents would think they were getting their dream daughter-in-law—another Muslim doctor in the fold—but instead they weren't exactly thrilled by his choice of wife. As I mentioned before, Safi is the second of four boys, and they'd wanted him to follow his older brother's lead by entering into an arranged marriage. Even though Safi had always told them that was never going to happen, they had never given up hope until I came into the picture. Now I was a living, breathing symbol of their unmet aspirations.

Also adding to our stress was that Safi's family are strict in their Islamic faith and my family is not. I could not expose my legs or even my elbows around my future in-laws due to their religious beliefs. I had once worn a strapless dress to my friend's wedding, and I had to hide that picture whenever they were in town so they wouldn't be offended. Safi and I could not order a beer with dinner like we usually would. It all felt so dishonest and disheartening.

It was something we'd work through slowly, and today we all have a great deal of love and respect for each other, thanks to our daughter Soraya. But at the time, we found ourselves at an impossible impasse: Safi's parents would not approve of any music, dancing, or alcohol at our wedding. And what were the things on my list of nonnegotiables? Music and dancing, and I also felt pretty strongly about having alcohol available for people who chose to drink it.

In the end, Safi and I brainstormed a way to make everyone happy, including ourselves. It was the first of many times to come that we used our collective problem-solving skills to overcome what seemed like insurmountable challenges. It would soon become our superpower.

Our compromise was to have two very distinct weddings on the same day. The first was a traditional Muslim ceremony. This sweet and serious affair was attended by all of Safi's people as well as my closest family members. The Imam who officiated was a younger guy—less traditional, welcoming, and warmer than I expected—who knew about and was fully supportive of our plan, so I figured we must be doing something right.

After a three-hour break—during which all of Safi's family left—we had another wedding, this one a nontraditional, joyous, and loud celebration of our love that included my extended family and all our friends. I wore a beautiful orange sari. Both Safi and I walked my dad down the aisle to Rusted Root and the Postal Service in celebration of the miracle that he was still alive after all he'd been through. I had bridesmen along with bridesmaids. The reception included plenty of music, dancing, and alcohol. Everyone had a blast.

The day turned out to be everything we wanted it to be. What made it even more special was how we made up our own rules. It's a tradition we continue to this day and another one of our superpowers. We do what's right for us, not what other people think we should do. Judgment has no place in our lives, then or now.

Once we'd committed our lives to one another, it was back to work for both of us. Safi returned to his residency in Toledo, and I continued in my rotations. We soon settled into our busy life, made busier by the fact that my father was hospitalized eight more times during the first few months of our marriage. He was now prone to bacterial infections of the bile duct, so one minute he'd be totally fine and the next he'd have a high fever, be septic, and get admitted to the intensive care unit. There were multiple episodes where we almost lost him.

49

Follow You into the Dark

Luckily, Henry Ford Hospital in Detroit, where he always ended up, isn't far from Toledo. It became our second home. Between the never-ending medical crisis and our crazy demanding jobs, we were still sleeping on an air mattress months after getting married.

Ironically, my first "rotation" with my dad was over before it ever got started due to his health issues. Despite the circumstances, it hadn't been a total wash. I'd certainly achieved the goal of spending more quality time with him, we'd grown closer as a result (Hey, I got my first *I love you!*), and I'd learned much more than a regular rotation would have provided me just from watching the medical staff respond to his ever-evolving and volatile situation. Truly, it had been quite an education.

My next rotation was at a hospital in nearby South Bend, this time focusing on pediatrics. Another irony: at the time, I had never considered going into the specialty. In fact, the reason I'd chosen the placement was because I *knew* I wasn't going into pediatrics ("peds"). My main motivation was that it was close to home and offered an easier schedule than most of the other available options. I'd wanted a low-pressure placement in the month leading up to my wedding, but what I got was so much more than that. There was so much kindness and compassion that seemed to accompany working with kids and their families.

I ended up loving every second of my peds rotation, but I didn't put too much weight into my reaction. I assumed it came more from no longer being stuck in a Detroit hospital room with my sick father than a true pull toward the specialty itself. I wasn't yet connecting the dots that I've always been inextricably drawn to children—I started babysitting at a young age, was a camp counselor, and always volunteered to tutor younger students—and that my medical practice would naturally come to specialize in treating them. There is just something about the innocence of children and the way they look at life that I've always found irresistible.

50

Keep Your Head Up

Instead, I decided to focus my attention on something even more life-changing than switching my specialty after years of being set on a different one: having my own child. I'd always known I wanted to be a mom. For as long as I could remember, I'd envisioned holding my own child. Hugging a child. Raising a child. Even when I thought about becoming a doctor, it was always through the lens of fitting it in with being a mother. My choice of specialty was based specifically on wanting a family. I thought, *I'll be a family doctor because they don't have to operate or be on call as much so I can be more present for my kids.*

Unfortunately for our baby-making plans, Safi and I had jam-packed work schedules and we were rarely in the same place at the same time. My rotations that year and the next were located all over the Midwest. And while most were in Toledo, there were also months I was commuting to Detroit an hour each way or living in Cleveland or Ann Arbor and coming home only on the weekends. Safi is also very practical and wanted to make sure I got accepted for residency in Toledo before bringing a baby into the picture. Our family expansion plans were put on hold as we focused on our careers.

After my peds rotation, I moved into a family medicine placement, my intended specialty. Of course I was fully expecting it to be my favorite. Pretty quickly, though, I realized I was skimming the schedule every morning to see how many kids were on it. They were always the highlight of my day. Yet I *still* didn't think much of my reaction other than *I really like working with kids, but of course I like working with adults, too.*

Next, I did an obstetrics and gynecology rotation. What I loved: delivering babies—I was often so excited about the newborn that had just arrived I forgot there was still a placenta to deliver. What I hated: any type of gyn surgery, and most especially the IUFDs (intrauterine fetal demise). I just couldn't stomach it. Every time I saw one listed on the labor and delivery board—where there was usually only happy news written, such as how far apart an expecting mother's contractions were or how much she was dilated—a part of me would die along with that stillborn baby. I always thought, *No, I am not going in there. I can't do it.* Clearly ob/gyn was not going to be the specialty for me.

After that, I rotated into child psych. I fell in love with it, probably with a fervor equal to the one I'd had for peds. Helping those kids and their families meant so much to me, maybe because I could relate to their difficulties after suffering from a deep depression just a few years earlier.

Really thinking about each of these rotations solidified my decision to become a pediatrician, which was in compliance with my National Health Service Corp Scholarship, so I applied to a pediatrics residency at a community hospital in Toledo and joined their latest cohort. Even though the program wasn't terribly competitive in terms of acceptances, I knew I could make the placement work to my advantage. Growing up in a tiny town yet still earning my way into a top-notch college had proven that education is what you make of it. I decided to give it my all in that small hospital and quickly started making a name for myself there.

Once again, Safi and I were making up our own rules as we went along. Knowing I was a well-respected, highly valued member of our class helped me feel safe about trying for a baby as an intern, which is rare due to the demanding 80-plus hour work week.

One of my biggest fears in life up to that point was not being able to be a mom. I'd thought about it all the time, even as a teenager. Every time I uttered a word about a future child, I'd always add *well, if I can have one.* I didn't ever want to assume something so beautifully large and life changing as becoming a parent was a given, and my acknowledgment felt like the equivalent of knocking on wood.

By my early twenties, my medical training had only served to heighten my paranoia about fertility. I saw so many people who tried everything under the sun to conceive but still could not, and I imagined the same thing happening to me on an endless loop. I constantly played out all kinds of scenarios in my mind: at what age would I be ready to become a mother? What would the quality of my eggs be at that point? What if my husband's sperm wasn't viable? I wanted a child so badly, I convinced myself it couldn't possibly happen—even the *thought* of being a mother felt too good to be true.

Luckily, all that worry was for naught. I got pregnant quickly, much to our great mutual joy. I surprised my parents with the exciting news by giving them a picture of my six-week ultrasound. They were thrilled for us and absolutely over the moon at the thought of becoming grandparents.

A week later, I was starting a long shift when I noticed some spotting. My senior resident was a man, so I didn't feel comfortable telling him about it—or the pregnancy. I hadn't revealed the news to anyone but my parents, and I certainly wasn't about to start now. Despite my concerns, I put my head down and kept right on working.

Thirty hours later when my shift was over, I called my obstetrician. She told me to meet her upstairs on the ob/gyn floor for an ultrasound. As soon as she squirted the cold gel on my stomach and began pushing that wand around my belly, her face dropped. I knew then that I'd lost the baby.

I sobbed all the way to my car. I was afraid to tell my parents because I felt even worse for them than I did for myself. We'd been through so much difficulty already, and I didn't want to contribute to our troubles with some more terrible news. I finally gathered up my courage and made the call. My parents were extremely supportive, although of course they shared in my disappointment. I resolved to protect them—and my own heart—more carefully next time.

Safi was at the Mayo Clinic in Minnesota doing an away rotation in hand surgery. He had once again gotten a deferment—the navy needed a hand surgeon, so it was in their best interest to allow him to complete his training before deploying him anywhere—so he had been busy shopping around for a fellowship. Safi ended up telling his attending physician (basically, his boss) at Mayo what was happening, and that sweet man bought Safi a ticket home so he could come be with me. When interviewing for medical training, it's usually all about trying to show people *all I care about is my job, I'm in it to win it*, so the Mayo Clinic's response was beautiful and unexpected.

The miscarriage left me totally devastated. Even though I was only seven weeks along in the pregnancy, it was crazy how much my connection to and love for that baby had grown during that short amount of time. My doctor later told me studies show that fetal loss is felt just as significantly whether it happens early or later in a pregnancy. Adding to my grief was that I'd worried so long about infertility, now this felt like proof my biggest fear was coming true. My only consolation was that I had gotten pregnant in the first place. I kept telling myself, *My body can do this. I can do this.*

Together, Safi and I let the disappointment and sadness sink in. It washed over us and then, like a tide, made its way back out into the sea of regrets. We recognized then—as we do now—that running away from hard emotions is never the answer.

After it felt like enough time had passed, we got back to the goal at hand: making babies. Again, I got pregnant quickly. Because I regretted telling my parents so early the last time, I was a lot more cautious about sharing my excitement. I kept our happy news to myself until what I considered to be a "safe" amount of time.

In the meantime, I celebrated this baby by deciding I was going to eat Cold Stone ice cream every single day of my pregnancy. I was like, *I earned it! I'm alive, this baby is alive, and this is definitely happening this time.* I also vowed not to exercise again until after I'd given birth. I'd taken a spin class a few days before I miscarried, I was concerned the two may have been somehow connected, and wasn't taking any chances. (I came to regret both decisions, by the way—my normally tiny stature was not made for 72 pounds of weight gain!)

Despite my elation about being pregnant, the actual day-to-day reality of it was not the absolute joy I expected it to be. I wondered why everyone said they loved it so much, because there was absolutely nothing beautiful about it to me. I was always nauseous. I developed sciatica, so my legs would often go numb during my marathon shifts. I had pinched nerves that made my back and neck ache mightily. I was downright exhausted all the time.

It hit me then that things don't often turn out like we expect them to. I'd been convinced I wouldn't be able to conceive, yet I'd already done it twice. I'd imagined if I ever got so lucky as to conceive it would be the most magical time of my life, and then it turned out to be constant puking, pins and needles in my legs, and a total pain in the neck.

Personal insight: I spent so much time worrying about whether I could get pregnant and planning the time to be pregnant that I never thought about miscarriage. When I actually had a miscarriage I never thought about what that loss would feel like or even that I would feel loss! When I got pregnant again, I never thought about being healthy while being pregnant as I was so cautious to *stay* pregnant. I also never thought about how hard it would be to be pregnant and be a resident. I tried so hard to plan and prepare . . . and none of it really mattered.

Universal takeaway: We can have the most meticulous plans organized down to the very last detail, and the universe will frequently have other ideas for us.

55

Follow You into the Dark

Chapter 8

Welcome to Your Life

I worked 80 hours a week right up until the end of my pregnancy. On the baby's due date, I received the hospital's Intern of the Year award—all my hard work and dedication had paid off—and two days later, I was in labor. After a routinely hard but rather uneventful delivery, Safi and I had ourselves a happy, healthy little girl.

We were ready with a list of names we liked. Safi's top pick was Yasmeen. I loved it but had a few others in contention as well, my favorite of which was Soraya. When I started worrying about what my mom would think if I named my firstborn after a friend—like maybe I was being silly and immature—I crossed it off as a possibility. Yasmeen it was.

Following our pattern of making up our own rules as we went along, Safi and I decided to institute a tradition of letting our siblings pick our children's middle names. We chose my sister as the beneficiary this time around. After some thought, she dubbed her Zara.

Little Yasmeen Zara was everything we could have hoped for: smart, curious, feisty, and strong. She was our little miracle from heaven here on earth. The embodiment of everything I'd ever dreamed of and more.

And yet.

While our baby was happy and healthy in the weeks and months following her birth, I was not faring quite as well. Postpartum depression rolled in and clouded all the joy that should have accompanied the welcome addition to our family. I got mad at the world for not telling me how difficult pregnancy, labor, delivery, and young mother-hood could be.

Once again, my expectations were not matching reality. I felt miserable and exhausted all the time. I was dealing with an incredibly painful second-degree tear, which was taking its time to heal. Breastfeeding did not come naturally, but I was still trying so hard to make it work that my nipples bled.

"Mom, why didn't you tell me I'd be leaking from every orifice of my body?!" I wailed to her one night as Yasmeen struggled to latch on.

She had no answer, of course. Mom only ever wants things to be happy. It's her coping mechanism, and it's gotten her this far in life, so I guess it works for her.

Managing family—my expectations of them and their expectations of me—was just another issue I hadn't anticipated before then. I'd wanted my mom and sister in the delivery room, but Safi argued that if his mom wouldn't be there, neither could they. It was a fair point, but I still didn't love the outcome, which meant both our families were stationed outside in the waiting room instead of me having my trusty support system by my side during the birth. I also wanted my mom and sister to help me out with everything after Yasmeen came, but when Safi's parents arrived, I grabbed her and hid in my room. I was desperate to get the hang of breastfeeding, and that meant having a lot of skin exposed. Between my in-laws' religious beliefs and my embarrassment at the thought of them seeing me half naked, there was no way I was comfortable sharing that experience with them. In the end, no one was happy with any of these arrangements, most especially me.

My maternity leave ended just five weeks postpartum—another decision I don't recommend. I'd chosen the extremely truncated time frame because it was the longest I could take off work and still stay with my residency cohort. If I extended my leave even a day longer, when I returned everyone else would have moved on to their third year while I remained a second-year resident. I'd already been left behind once before in med school, and I had no intention of doing it again.

My early transition back to work was far harder than I expected, just as becoming a mother had been. Walking the tightrope between working as many hours as I needed to as a resident and being the present and loving mother I aspired to felt damn near impossible. Finding the right daycare seemed like a life-or-death decision, and I had pangs of guilt and worry whenever I dropped Yasmeen off in someone else's care no matter how qualified they were. Even things as formerly simple as getting to work on time became a big deal. Breastfeeding still hadn't gotten any easier.

"Just give her formula," Safi told me one early morning as I sobbed trying to get enough calories into Yasmeen before I went to work.

"I can't, I'm a pediatrician!" I cried.

The pressure I put on myself to perform perfectly in all areas of my life was enormous, and motherhood was no exception. I once counted all the times I spent pumping milk to ensure I had enough available for Yasmeen's nutritional needs, and it came to 24 hours a week. I set alarms to pump in the middle of the night. I pumped in the call room at work. I'd see patients, maybe do a spinal tap or two, and then go pump some more. I couldn't fathom telling the new moms in my practice they should breastfeed for at least six months if possible and then not do it myself. So I refused to give up despite the difficulty and lack of enjoyment both of us were experiencing in the process. I practically killed myself trying to make it work, yet it never did.

Throughout it all, I kept reminding myself how lucky I was to have a happy, healthy baby. Yasmeen had a strict schedule for bed-time, sleeping, and feeding. She wasn't fussy. She didn't get sick very often. She loved her childcare provider. I simply couldn't imagine

Welcome to Your Life

how parents with anything less than a "perfect" baby like Yasmeen ever left the house, much less held down a job.

I'd seen my fair share of complex kids in training, and it always confounded me how their parents seemed so well-adjusted despite the difficult circumstances. Many even told me, *This child is the best thing that ever happened to me. If I had to, I would do this over and over again.*

At the time, all I could think was *these parents are angels; there's no way I could do that.* I had so many biases I didn't recognize back then. If I could revisit that period—knowing what I know now and everything we've been through since—I would talk to those parents more about their experiences and ask how long it had taken them to get to such a joyous realization about their special needs children. I still haven't quite gotten to the "I would pick this over and over again for us," but maybe I will someday.

Of course, Safi and I had all sorts of hopes for Yasmeen's future: She would get straight As in school. She'd participate in sports. She'd go to a great college. We were determined she would live out our dream of what it looks like to be a successful, healthy child.

Looking back, it's embarrassing how much I believed I controlled all those things. The fact that Yasmeen went along with the plan only magnified my belief that parents have a say in how their kids grow and who they become. I know better now.

Safi continued interviewing for his hand surgery fellowship after his abrupt departure from the Mayo Clinic. Because I still had a year left in my residency, his goal was to find a program within driving distance of Toledo. We were gunning for one in Chicago, but in the end, he matched in Cincinnati.

At three hours away, it was not a tenable daily commute. We'd just have to have a long-distance marriage for a year, with Safi coming back to Toledo whenever his schedule allowed. Yasmeen was settled into her childcare and thriving there, and I'd just have to make it work as a single parent for the time being.

Safi was the first DO ever accepted into this particular fellowship—one of the best programs in the country for hand surgery—a testament both to his skill and work ethic. He'd rotated at the hospital as a resident, so they knew how talented he was. I was both in awe and proud of his accomplishment.

"Why don't you try to transfer residencies?" he suggested one night after we'd both come off long shifts.

Cincinnati Children's has one of the strongest pediatric programs in the country and is currently rated the number one pediatric hospital. Toledo is a community hospital, and the program I was in was small and noncompetitive. There's simply no comparison between the two. "There's no way they'll take me as a transfer!" I replied, interested but also resigned to the fact that it could never happen.

It's not like we hadn't considered the possibility of a transfer before. Another reason I'd gone back to work so quickly after having Yasmeen was so I could stay on the assigned academic calendar in case it became necessary to switch programs to stay with Safi. But transferring residencies in general is not a thing, especially as an entering third year going from a small community hospital to a large, prestigious, research-based academic institution like Cincinnati.

Our creative problem-solving superpowers to the rescue again! Safi cold emailed the lone DO faculty member at Cincinnati with his news of becoming the first DO ever in this hand surgery fellowship. At the end of his message, he also not-so-subtly included the rest of our story: we were both residents with a small child and this could be our only year together before he was deployed by the navy and me to the NHSC, so if there was anything anyone could do to help transfer my residency to Cincinnati Children's we'd greatly appreciate it.

To our amazement, that doctor immediately shot back a note congratulating Safi on his great accomplishment. In it, he also asked me to forward anything I'd published plus letters of recommendation to facilitate a possible transfer to the current program director. I could not even believe our luck—or how bittersweet the possibility of leaving would be.

Acquiring the requested letters of recommendation meant I'd need to be transparent with my current program about my intentions. I loved the relationships I'd made in Toledo and how supported and successful I'd been there. I was the first person in my class that year to be published and was recognized for my efforts as top intern of the year. I'd greatly enjoyed being a big fish in a little pond, so telling my program director and chief residents was gut-wrenching. While they were disappointed, they understood why I was considering leaving and were on board with my decision to pursue a transfer.

As a result of my strong work ethic and success in that little community hospital, my recommendations were stellar. I had publications that provided further proof of my abilities and ambition. As a result, I was offered an interview at Cincinnati Children's Hospital.

I'm going to let you in on a little secret here: I'd originally applied for a residency there back when I was still in med school and never even made it past stage one. I didn't even get a rejection—it was just crickets. Now, because of the large impact I'd been able to have in a small program, I was being considered as a viable candidate, much like how being an excellent student back in my hometown of Dowagiac had gotten me into a prestigious college.

So much of what happened next was the result of being in the right place at the right time. First, a person in the program was skipping his last year of residency and going directly into a fellowship, so there was an opening for a third-year pediatric resident. Because these positions are funded in advance, it's not like programs can add people on a whim. There is a strict number of spots, and that's that.

This supersmart resident moving into the next phase of his training a year early left a spot in the program exactly where I needed one. It was nothing short of a miracle, which we've had many more of since.

The actual interview turned out to be just as serendipitous. The chair of the program asked me about my hometown, and I said I'd grown up in Dowagiac. As it turned out, his sister lived on the same street there as my best friend and his nephew was friends with my older brother. I think this shared connection may have just clinched the deal for me.

In the end, I was offered the position and accepted it gratefully. Safi, Yasmeen, and I were staying together like we'd hoped. After that, whenever I ran into that resident who accelerated his education in the hospital, I always felt the need to express my appreciation to him. I'd say something like "I'd like to thank you for allowing me to have your spot in the residency program and letting our family stay together." It was kind of awkward, but I wanted him to know just how much he'd affected our lives.

Hard work, dedication, and determination always seemed to find a way to pay us back with dividends.

Personal insight: We didn't settle on the idea of being apart in my last year of residency. We reached out, took chances, and were prepared for rejections. Never would I have imagined that it would work out to be together.

Universal takeaway: Color outside the lines. When there doesn't seem to be a solution to a problem that has been tried and true, create something new and try it.

Chapter 9

It's Quiet Uptown

As with most things in life, there were some difficult developments that came along with our great fortune. Going from a small residency program of 8 people to a big academic one of 50 was rough for me. While I made the most of the education and resources only a top teaching hospital can provide for the single year I was there, I'd once again lost the camaraderie of a class I'd grown close to. I was absorbed into a new and unfamiliar one, and without the benefit of shared history, I had no sense of belonging.

I decided then that maybe I just hadn't found exactly where I belonged in this world yet. Perhaps I was meant to flit about the edges like I had been until the right opportunity presented itself. Little did I know it would come with an extremely high price of admission, paid in great personal pain, the beginnings of which were brewing at that very moment.

Safi soon found out he was being stationed in Virginia after his fellowship was over. The good news: it was a domestic placement that would allow us to continue to stay together as a family. The bad news: the only site within driving distance of his job that qualified for the terms of my four-year commitment to NHSC was not in need of a pediatrician at that time.

This called for more creative problem-solving on our part. Safi scheduled an appointment with the medical executive officer at the NHSC qualifying practice, then flew in for the meeting wearing his full dress military uniform. Once there, he resorted to begging them to make space for me. His pitch was: my wife will work full-time for reduced pay. Again, luck was on our side. I was hired.

Now that we knew we had a home base for four years, we felt more settled than ever before. Yes, there was the possibility Safi could get deployed during that time, but if that happened, he'd return to our home in Virginia once it was over. Knowing we'd be staying put for an extended period, Safi and I decided it was time to get back to baby making.

Before Yasmeen came along, Safi and I thought two or three children would be the perfect number for our family. Once we had a child and started realizing that balancing parenthood and our careers was going to be much harder than we expected, we ratcheted the "maybe three" plan back down to a solid two. Knowing this would be my last pregnancy, I decided to take a more balanced and sane approach this time.

Nature once again did its job quickly, much to our joy and delight. Immediately, everything seemed nicer and more controlled than during our first go-round. I knew my body could sustain a pregnancy, so I wasn't fearful of a miscarriage. Rather than putting in 80 hours a week like I had as a resident, I was now working far more reasonable hours in an outpatient setting. I was finally exercising, faithfully walking and doing yoga, and I substituted Greek yogurt for my former daily Cold Stone habit—there was no way I was letting myself gain 72 pounds again. If this baby didn't take to breastfeeding, I decided I wasn't going to push so hard to make it work. And perhaps most important, I knew five weeks of maternity leave was not nearly enough, so I was going to take a much more reasonable 10 to 12 weeks. Things were going along swimmingly.

Still, there were some moments that perhaps should have given us more pause than they did early on. Given how planful we'd been, we knew exactly when this baby was conceived. Yet our first ultrasound showed a different result.

66

Keep Your Head Up

When the OB gave me the baby's due date, I corrected her. "It's actually a week earlier."

"Well, that's what you're measuring," she replied, adding, "sometimes people are wrong about the conception date."

I thought, *She's wrong, I'm right. I know exactly when I conceived.* But if the OB wasn't worried about it, I figured I shouldn't be either. Still, that week difference was always in the back of my mind throughout the pregnancy, an itch I never could quite scratch.

I'm thankful I didn't look up what it could mean at the time, because I would have learned it is a big red flag. Very early on, ultrasound due dates are spot-on and become less accurate as a pregnancy gets farther along. Five days off is enough of a differential to set off alarms, and mine was seven days off. Unfortunately, my doctor had already decided I was mistaken about when the baby was conceived and dismissed this discrepancy as any cause for worry.

Complicating our journey was the fact that if a woman is not of "advanced maternal age" (usually defined as over 35) and has no history of complicated childbirth, the military only allows for half the number of doctors' visits as a civilian receives. Since I was only 33 at the time and had no preexisting conditions that would necessitate more frequent monitoring, I had relatively few check-ins with my OB. They didn't even have me pee in a cup!

Still, we did get certain perks and more attentive care than we otherwise would have because Safi was an attending physician in the military. For instance, my OB agreed to deliver our baby as a courtesy—attending physician to attending physician—rather than whoever happened to be on call when the time came. She found and prescribed me a medicine for migraines safe to take during pregnancy and offered me a magnetic resonance imaging just to make sure everything was okay. And at about the 30-week mark, she found that I was still measuring smaller than even the week-off due date, so she did an ultrasound weekly from there on out. Everything always looked okay.

I went into labor at what the doctor assumed was 38 weeks but was really 39. As the baby's heart rate kept decelerating, we started considering a C-section. I was willing to do it, but I felt like the OB made her preference for the natural route crystal clear. I wanted to do whatever was healthiest and safest for the baby, and I figured she knew best.

There was a lot of back-and-forth, but by the time the doctor had me consent for a C-section, I was already 10 centimeters dilated. There was no time left. I gave one push, and the baby was out.

There was an immediate silence. I saw Safi's face and knew those weren't happy tears running down his cheeks. I could tell the baby wasn't moving the right side of her body, and all of a sudden, an entire team of people rushed in.

The only thing I could think in that moment was that this wasn't about me anymore. It was about our tiny little Soraya, whose life seemed to be hanging in the balance. I wasn't worried anymore what my mom might think of us naming her after her best friend (who had given us her permission to do so, I might add). I didn't care what Safi's brother Hameed decided her middle name would be (it turned out to be Zaina). I just wanted her to live.

I didn't know exactly what was wrong, I just knew how wrong it all felt. Where there should have been cheers of joy, a dull silence filled the room.

Safi tried to offer me some comforting words, but I felt like I already understood more about what was going on than he did. Soraya's due date had never been off; it was simply that she hadn't grown at the proper rate and now had big problems as a result. Whatever was happening to my baby wouldn't be fixed in an instant, that much I knew for sure.

"You go with her," I told Safi as our baby was whisked off to the neonatal intensive care unit. "I don't need you to be here with me. She needs you now."

No one said a thing to me in that moment, and it felt like I'd tacitly agreed to not knowing the details of what was going on because I wasn't asking any questions. I just trusted everyone was giving the best care possible to my baby and that Safi would get all the information we needed to move forward. I also knew he would get our baby back to me as fast as possible once she was stabilized.

When Soraya was finally returned to me, she was still on monitors but seemed to be doing okay. Even though I'd carried her to term, she weighed only 5 pounds, 14 ounces, which was considered small for gestational age. She just looked so tiny and helpless; it was hard not to consider the difficulties her future might hold.

In our first picture with Soraya, Safi and I are both crying. It was a worried cry though, not one of triumph. I still couldn't have that moment of joy every new mother anticipates. This sounds awful, but there was no joy to be found that day. Joy was absent from that room. Everything was solemn and so terribly quiet.

When Yasmeen arrived with the friend who was watching her, our family felt complete. Now we could call our extended family and recount the frightening arrival of our new daughter, Soraya. Of course they were happy for us, but it was of a much more subdued nature.

There was thankfully some good news that day: Soraya latched on and nursed well right away. Unfortunately, there was also more bad news: she seemed to get tired quickly and never lasted for very long. Her tone felt floppy, and her movements seemed uncoordinated. Nothing about her felt right, but I couldn't quite put my finger on what the exact problem was.

I started asking the pediatrician some pointed questions when she came to check in on us. "Why is she small for gestational age? I carried her to term, so it doesn't make sense," I began.

"You're petite and your husband's on the smaller side. It's just genetics," she replied confidently.

At the time, I felt reassured. Looking back, though, I should have known there was no logical reason why my second baby would be that much smaller than the first. Each baby in subsequent pregnancies should be bigger because the uterus gets bigger with each one.

"But why is she getting so tired when she's feeding?" I continued.

"Newborns are tired. You'll just have to wake her up some more," she told me, dismissing my concerns just like my OB had.

Soraya wanted to nurse constantly, which felt like a hopeful sign. But she was also fussy and irritable all the time. She made weird noises when she was feeding. I was left wondering, *What is going on with you, little baby?*

At Soraya's two-week appointment, she was still gaining weight just fine. When I mentioned my concerns to the doctor—the floppy tone, the unusual noises—the pediatrician blamed everything on the fact that I was studying for my medical boards, a notoriously hard test doctors must take to get licensed. She presumed it was making me overthink Soraya's health.

"If I were to refer you to ENT [ear, nose, and throat] right now, they would laugh you out of the office," she told me. "There's absolutely nothing to worry about."

Because she was married to one of Safi's higher-ups, I accepted her further dismissal without another word. I didn't want to ruffle her feathers because her husband's rank meant he had a direct say in where and when Safi would be deployed. No way was I messing with that power dynamic.

As Soraya's fussiness continued, she was diagnosed with reflux, and we got her on medicine to help calm her symptoms. Oddly, though, her struggles while nursing only increased. We had to keep her upright for at least half an hour after she ate, or she would scream and vomit. Constant rocking was the only thing that could begin to console her.

Even more concerning was the fact that I couldn't get her to take a bottle, and there was no way I'd be able to go back to work full-time until she did. My mom flew out to see us, determined to do a "bottle boot camp." She thought she would be able to get Soraya in line quickly. I dutifully went out every day Mom was there—she said it would be an easier fix if I wasn't around—but whenever I came home, nothing had changed. Mom had been so determined, but she had been defeated.

"I'm so sorry I couldn't get her to do it," she sadly told me before she left to go back home.

Soraya's confounding feeding and reflux problems continued to be upsetting. So was her lack of muscle control. I kept telling Safi, "I don't think her tone is right."

"Do you want me to take her to my orthopedic colleagues just to see?" he offered after I said it for what must have seemed like the hundredth time since she was born.

"Yes, please."

We again got reassurance from other doctors, but I just could not shake the feeling that something was really wrong with our beautiful second-born child.

I was even starting to wonder when—if ever—things would become "normal" in our world again.

Personal insight: In reflection, there were so many "pink flags" of things that just didn't feel right. I couldn't put my finger on it and neither could her doctors. Not letting my intuition go was key to getting her the medical support she needed.

Universal takeaway: Trust your gut. When you get an inkling of anything within yourself medically or for your child, listen to it and say something. Stay curious. Keep asking the questions and sharing your fears.

Chapter 10

Cherub Rock

At Soraya's two-month visit, my pediatrician assured me, "She'll take a bottle once she gets to daycare. She can refuse it now because she knows you're here to breastfeed her. She won't have that option once you go back to work, and she certainly won't starve herself."

I wasn't so sure. I couldn't imagine a daycare worker having any more luck bottle-feeding Soraya than my mom or I had, especially given the upright rocking necessary to avoid her desperate grunting and tendency to throw up after being fed. In fact, I was pretty sure daycare was not in the cards for this baby, at least for the time being.

Desperate to find another appropriate alternative, I started going on a popular, well-regarded website, searching for the best caregiver for Soraya. My plan was to employ a nanny until she was able to take a bottle well and then give daycare a try. Yasmeen was thriving there, we loved the program, and they'd promised to save a spot for Soraya for when she was ready. *If* she was ever ready, that is.

I'd never gone on this site before, but I was convinced it was the best option. I liked the fact that the caregivers listed there were both certified and background checked. When I clicked on the profile of a young woman who was doing online college for criminal justice and wanted to become a police officer, I decided she was the one. Her two references—one was a police officer, and another was a parent—gave her rave reviews, instilling even more confidence in my choice.

Safi and I asked her to come to our home for an interview, and this young woman continued to impress us with her self-confidence and high aspirations. She had a small child of her own, so we told her she could bring her baby to our home while she was caring for Soraya. The only thing we asked in return was for her to keep their toys separate so they were not teething on the same things. We also pointed out a couple of toys that are really special to our family and asked that her child not play with those. As for everything else in the house, she had free rein.

We understood she was trying to better herself, so we told her she was free to study while the kids were napping. I even offered her the use of my computer while she was in our home to make things easier for her. She eagerly accepted our offer to do a trial for a couple of half days before I went back to work.

I was, of course, nervous about leaving Soraya with someone new, so I was very meticulous in my instructions as to how to hold and rock her while trying to get some bottle ounces in. The nanny commented, "You're very particular about how you like things done."

"That's true," I told her.

She said, "I imagine it's going to be really hard for you to go back to work."

I nodded. "True again."

"I see you have an iPhone," she continued. "I don't know if you're aware of this, but there are cameras you can get to check in on her while you're at work. You could have one in her room and one down here. That way you'll still be able to see Soraya during the day and know that she's okay."

I liked the idea but worried it wasn't affordable. "A nanny cam? Aren't they crazy expensive?"

"Actually, not so much anymore," she told me. "And I do think the expense is worth the extra peace it would give you."

I forgot about that conversation for the first few weeks I was back at work but mentioned it to Safi once I remembered. He was a bundle of enthusiasm. "That would be so great! I'd love to check in on Soraya during the day!"

He immediately ordered a camera, thinking we'd see how it went with one and get more if needed. It was delivered the following Friday and we installed it over the weekend. Monday was the beginning of our nanny's third week working for us, and she'd assured us Soraya had been taking her bottle during that time.

We both forgot to tell her we'd installed the nanny cam before leaving for work that day. I texted Safi later that morning about our oversight: *We totally forgot to tell her about the camera! Should I text her?*

Safi replied: *No, we'll just tell her when we get home. No need to make it into a big thing, it was her suggestion in the first place.*

That afternoon, Safi had a cancellation for surgery, and we started going back and forth about whether we should check the camera. It was just so tempting to see how well cared for our baby was and to confirm our belief that we'd done the right thing by choosing a nanny over daycare.

Still, I waffled: *What if she takes care of the babies topless? Remember how I did that when I was so desperate to get Yasmeen to breastfeed?*

We went back and forth texting: *You do it.*

No, you do it.

Finally, we decided it would not be an invasion of privacy to watch our daughter since the nanny had tacitly given us permission by suggesting we get the camera in the first place. We clicked on the app at the same time. What I saw made me sick to my stomach.

Soraya was in a swing screaming her head off while this woman was busy typing away on my computer. She wasn't even looking at my baby, no less comforting her—she just kept kicking the swing with her foot. Next, she grabbed one of the only two toys I asked her not to share with her child and gave it to the baby, who put it directly in their mouth. Next, she put my precious breast milk in the microwave and shoved the hot bottle into Soraya's mouth without even testing it and went back to kicking the swing.

I could barely breathe; I was so furious. "I'm going to get Soraya," I told Safi.

"Don't confront her because things could get violent," he advised. "Don't make any accusations. Do not say a word about this. Just tell her you got off work early and don't need her help. The two of us can talk to her later tonight about what we saw."

I was fuming and shaking by the time I got home, but somehow, I found the composure not to give this woman the piece of my mind she deserved. I told her I was going to take Soraya on some errands and left. I carried her in a BabyBjörn while seeing patients the rest of the day.

That night, Safi and I called the nanny on speakerphone. We explained that we'd gotten the camera per her suggestion, it was not our intent to keep that information from her, and that we'd both felt bad about watching it without her knowledge. She didn't say a word, so we continued.

"We saw you kicking the swing multiple times. We saw you use the toys we asked you not to. We saw you microwave breast milk that took so much work to pump."

She hung up on us before we could say any more and would not pick up when we tried to call her back multiple times. I still sent her last paycheck and her baby's toys that she'd left at our house, mostly because I felt bad for her baby. Then I called her references and told them about what happened. I made sure they knew I wasn't blaming them for the situation, but I wanted them to know in case they were called to vouch for her again. They were predictably mortified.

After that traumatizing experience, we immediately put Soraya into daycare. It was tried and true. I decided I would breastfeed her all night if that meant she'd be safe during the day. When I told the daycare workers what had happened, they cried along with me. They promised to take extra loving care of her, which they did beautifully.

Nonetheless, Soraya still would only take an ounce from the bottle at most during the day. The daycare was very concerned about not being able to feed her more, so I went there every day on my lunch break to nurse her. I nursed her again as soon as I picked her up. And then I nursed her throughout the night. It wasn't easy, but I'd do anything for my kids—even forgo sleep for the foreseeable future.

By this point, Soraya was three months old. She hadn't been weighed since her two-month well visit, at which point she was still gaining weight at a decent rate because she was breastfeeding full-time. At her three-month visit, we learned she wasn't gaining as well anymore, which wasn't a big surprise because we knew she wasn't getting much from the bottle at daycare. She'd also started getting sick all the time—multiple ear infections and even a bout of pneumonia—presumably from being exposed to all the other kids' germs.

We normalized the illnesses, thinking that's what you get when you sign up for daycare. We also got very adept at rationalizing: *she has pneumonia, it's okay, she must have gotten it from another kid in daycare. Oh, she's not gaining as much weight as she should? Must be because of her reflux, or because she's still not taking a bottle well, or because she's been too stuffy to eat as much as she needs to.*

By the four-month visit, these things became harder to justify. Soraya had really fallen off the curve. When a baby is that far off the growth chart, the diagnosis is most often failure to thrive. This triggers a workup or intervention to get the baby to gain weight.

As much as I wish that was the moment our pediatrician decided it was time to get Soraya evaluated, that's not what happened. The doctor instead suggested we give solid foods a try to chunk Soraya up. The approach didn't make much sense to me, but I didn't have the energy to fight her on it. After spending the past four months thinking *something's wrong* on a loop, I was more than happy to change my refrain to *this is normal. We'll just get some more food into her, and she'll be fine.*

Still, I already had a suspicion this was just wishful thinking on our part. In my observations of Soraya taking the bottle, she was still terribly uncoordinated. Everything was a struggle. It didn't seem like *I just don't want to take the bottle because it's not your breast.* I felt like I could tell a difference between those two things in my gut, and that wasn't it.

I also worried about the possibility of Soraya choking on solid food because she still didn't have good head control. She was barely holding her head up independently, which is necessary to be able to chew and swallow food properly. Technically, babies should have no head lag by six months and hers was still lagging greatly.

Something in me must have known this wasn't going to end well, because I decided to take a video of the first time Soraya tried solid food. First came the choking. Next, a horrible, strangled, stridor noise like the kind that accompanies a serious croup attack. It sounded like she may have aspirated the food, but of course I couldn't be sure.

That was *the* moment. Everything suddenly tied together in a big sick bow, from the incorrect due date to the scary delivery to the gut feelings I'd had ever since. I didn't know what was wrong, but I did know my life as I knew it was over.

Soraya's life as I knew it was over.

Personal insight: When I decided to get the nanny cam, it was a struggle for me to push myself to get it and then even harder to watch. I really tried to talk myself out of it. I am so grateful I followed through to witness what happened. It had to be done to keep Soraya safe.

Similarly, I kept trying to reassure myself that Soraya was fine medically when *I knew* something was off. It was a struggle of two forces: the medical reassurance versus my intuition.

Universal takeaway: When you get a gut feeling about something—don't dismiss it. When you ignore your intuition, sometimes the universe will command your attention.

Chapter 11

Ways to Go

I couldn't explain exactly what was happening, but I understood how serious the situation was. I'd already concluded: this is a child who is going to need all sorts of therapies: physical therapy, occupational therapy, speech therapy, feeding therapy, the works. The road ahead for Soraya would not be an easy one.

I texted the video to the pediatrician and demanded she order a swallow study for us. She immediately complied, giving me the phone number I needed to schedule an appointment. Of course, there were no openings until a full month later, leaving me plenty of time to sit and stew about what the problem might be.

I developed a theory that Soraya might have an anatomical issue where the heart constricts the esophagus, making it hard to swallow. I thought the study would be able to determine the problem and then she would have surgery to fix it. The recovery might be long, but everything would be fine.

Still, waiting a whole month for the study was terrifying. I just tried to be grateful Soraya was still alive. I couldn't put my fear into words because I didn't even know what I was afraid of, so I needed constant reassurance. My family and friends were only too happy to give it to me. I'd say, "I just feel like something's off" and they'd go into a spiel about how Soraya was in daycare and probably sounded like that on the video because she'd caught yet another cold.

When we finally went in for the swallow study, I insisted both Safi and I had to be there. I held Soraya and fed her a bottle while technicians took multiple X-rays to see exactly how and where the milk was going. I was not expecting immediate results, but the radiologist came out to speak to us before the bottle was even halfway done.

"I need to talk to you. Your baby is aspirating," he told us. "You have a long road ahead."

Those words knocked the wind right out of me. That one single sentence encapsulated everything I'd been thinking since Soraya's birth. Suddenly, the pneumonia, the frequent fevers, and the fussiness all made sense. Yes, Soraya had reflux, but there was also a bigger problem: all that fluid we were force-feeding her was going straight into her lungs, and it freaking hurt her. *That's* why she wouldn't take a bottle. *That's* why she screamed after we fed her. *That's* why she made those unsettling noises.

My heart started hammering away in my chest. "What do we need to do?" I asked.

He started ticking off a giant list of things. "You're going to need to see multiple subspecialists to find out why she's aspirating. You'll have to arrange for numerous therapies to get her to feed correctly. There's a great rehab doctor you should consult with to determine how to move forward in the most effective manner."

Already, overwhelm was setting in. We'd just gotten the sobering message of how difficult this journey was going to be, and now we were facing an incredibly time-consuming battle to right what we already knew was going wrong. Not to mention, we still had to find out why these problems were happening in the first place!

We had scheduled a follow-up appointment with the pediatrician immediately after the swallow study. While I'd been angry from the moment I sent her the video, I'd managed to hold it all together during the swallow study, but now that we knew my baby was aspirating, I was completely flipping out. It felt like my world was being torn apart. I wanted to scream at anybody that got in my way, "I knew something was wrong!"

I needed someone to tell me what this could possibly be. The only diagnoses I could think of were incredibly bad. Some of them were only life-threatening diseases, but most were life-ending.

So, there I was on a Friday afternoon, in tears at our pediatrician's office, listing off the frightening symptoms our poor child was experiencing. "Her tone is off. She sweats while she feeds. She's making this horrible sound. She's aspirating," I told her. "What do you think this is and what are our next steps?"

She immediately went into colleague-to-colleague mode, which is not what any parent needs even if they are a fellow doctor. "My guess is that she has spinal muscular atrophy," she responded, her face going ashen. "I was just reading up on it for my board recertification. She has feeding difficulties, she's smaller for her age, she has low tone, and she has full head lag. Those are all the signs of it."

Spinal muscular atrophy (SMA) is essentially a death sentence, comparable to a super-aggressive baby amyotrophic lateral sclerosis. It is a progressive neurological disease that slowly weakens the muscles until breathing is no longer possible. When SMA is diagnosed before age one, the prognosis is death by age two. Just as of this year, there are newer drugs that have been shown to slow down the progress of the disease, but back then there was little hope for any child with this diagnosis.

In my head I was thinking, "How dare you go from 'she's fine' to SMA?!" Knowing I needed her help in that moment, though, I just nodded.

She took another look at five-and-a-half-month-old Soraya and exclaimed, "She really has no head strength at all, does she?"

I couldn't hold my tongue this time. "I've been telling you that for months! Now what are you going to do about it?"

Right then and there, the pediatrician finally diagnosed Soraya with failure to thrive. She referred us to a gastrointestinal doctor to investigate the cause of Soraya's malnutrition, help us figure out how to get her to gain weight, and see if there was reflux. We got another referral to genetics and yet another to rehab medicine to help Soraya learn how to eat without aspirating.

Then the pediatrician got on the phone, called a neurologist she knew personally, and played a "doctor card" to get us in to see him the very next day. She knew that, beyond all the drama we'd been dealing with in terms of Soraya's health, we had also gotten some other startling news recently: Safi was getting deployed to Afghanistan for an undetermined amount of time in a little over three months. I needed to get everything sorted out before he left, because I was going to be a single mom for the foreseeable future after that.

I remember sitting in the closet when I got home, sobbing as I called my best friends and family. I kept repeating, "She's going to die. I can't live through her dying!" They assured me the magnetic resonance imaging (MRI) the neurologist had ordered was simply to rule out the worst possible disease it could be, but there was no way Soraya had it.

Safi and I somehow made it through that night and got to the hospital the next day. The neurologist we'd been referred to was a seasoned, older doctor with a kind, calm demeanor. It seemed like nothing ever got him frazzled. "I am confident she doesn't have SMA," he reported back after examining Soraya and performing an MRI. "Her eyes are so bright!"

I could have thrown my arms around his neck and hugged him; I was so excited to hear the amazing news. I ended up hugging Safi instead. We were both crying happy tears.

"Honestly, her exam wasn't bad at all," the doctor continued. I'm sure the fact that he had been concerned enough to see us on a Saturday made him expect to see something very different in Soraya. "She's got some mild low tone, and you need to increase her calorie intake. Her head is big for her body, so you'll need a genetic workup and a battery of labs. Still, I am absolutely confident this is not SMA."

Finally, we'd been given a little ray of hope. Some peace. Maybe whatever Soraya had could still be "fixed."

Pretty soon, though, my relief turned into rage over how my doctor had so casually told me she thought my baby had a deadly disease. Because I was a physician, she took it on herself to speak to me like a physician and completely disregarded the fact that I was simply a mom fearing for my baby's life in that situation. How dare she send me home to sob all night because I thought my child was dying and I would have to bury her while Safi was in Afghanistan? Her choice of words went beyond disrespectful.

Something shifted in my mind in how I viewed her after that. Medicine has a distinct hierarchy, and, at the time, I was a newly graduated resident and she was an attending. From that moment forward, I considered us on equal footing. No longer would I hang on any other doctor's word and take it as gold—I was just as competent and knowledgeable as they were now.

My experience of having my concerns dismissed first by my OB and then by my pediatrician completely changed how I communicate with my patients. I understand the large impact my words have and am careful about what I say and the way in which I say it. I also make it a point to listen—truly listen—to every concern a parent has. If they are worried about anything, even if it's something seemingly benign—hiccups, for example—I hear them out instead of quickly dismissing the concern and even more quickly giving reassurance (which honestly a lot of pediatrics do—reassurance, validation, reassurance, validation).

As a result of my being dismissed by doctors, I am now always careful to ask, "Why are you worried about that? What do you think is going to happen? What is your fear in this?"

I take what they tell me and try to provide proof as to why they can stop worrying about it. So maybe it's something like, "There's no way they are going to choke and die because they've been gaining weight well, they've never aspirated, and they are good on the growth chart. Even if they did cough, it would save them, not kill them."

If a parent is still freaked out after all that, I offer to refer them to a specialist. I tell them, "I don't blame you for wanting to get reassurance from someone who is smarter than me. This may be a waste of time, but I think nothing is a waste of time if it lets you sleep at night."

In the end, people just want to be heard. I hadn't been given that courtesy and look where we were now: no closer to having an answer than when our sweet little baby was born.

She'd already been through so much pain, and there was still no end in sight.

Personal insight: The way that I was told that Soraya may have SMA is seared in my mind. I wish it came out with a kinder delivery than a casual conversation between colleagues. I also feel there were a series of concerns that were dismissed by my physicians. As a result of my being dismissed by doctors, I am now always careful to ask my own patients, "Why are you worried about that? What do you think is going to happen? What is your fear in this?"

Universal takeaway: For my fellow physicians, providers, caretakers: delivery matters! Know your words have an impact. Also, take time to listen and respond. Avoid empty reassurance. Respond in a way that directly addresses the concern.

Chapter 12

Nuthin' but a "G" Thang

So now we had some good news: at least Soraya didn't have spinal muscular atrophy. However, the feeding difficulties, frequent illnesses, muscular incoordination, lack of weight gain, and constant pain continued unabated no matter what we did.

The ever-expanding list of doctors and specialists we'd been told to consult had zero answers regarding what could be causing Soraya's health problems. Everything she was tested for came back negative. Her labs didn't reveal any big red flags. Neurology—whom we assumed would be our salvation in finding a diagnosis—was at an equal loss. It was incomprehensible that no one had a clue how to help our beautiful little girl.

A woman I knew from residency happened to be in town, so she came over for a visit. We'd rotated together before we solidified our specialties, and she was now a neurologist. Suddenly, I wasn't looking at her as a friend so much anymore but as a lifeline. "Tell me anything you think it could be!" I pleaded with her. "What should we be looking for?"

She patiently explained to me everything the doctors were checking into and why. It was nice to have medical reassurance that we weren't missing anything. It was also a big relief to know she thought our doctors were running through all the right assessments and possibilities.

The next few weeks were a whirlwind of ever more tests and therapies. By the time the gastroenterologist was up to bat, we'd already been to so many appointments that I felt perfectly capable of handling this one without Safi. I thought, *It's just about nutrition. How hard can it be?*

At the time, it seemed like an incredibly low-stakes visit given the other specialties we'd already seen. I assumed the doctor would order more testing and offer instructions on how to feed Soraya supplemental, higher-calorie foods. No big deal.

I even had a point of connection with this physician, giving me an extra boost of confidence. When I was a med student, I rotated in gastro-intestinal (GI) for a month at the Cleveland Clinic. I loved my attending physician there—he often gave me articles to read and then quizzed me on them later, an extra bit of teaching he didn't have to do that I so appreciated—and his fellow at the time was the GI doctor we were now scheduled to see. While I didn't expect him to remember me (medical students are like peons to fellows), I certainly felt comfortable enough to send him an email requesting a fast-tracked appointment since Safi's deployment was rapidly approaching. He obliged and moved our meeting up to Halloween.

Of course, I had already bought adorable costumes for the girls and was looking forward to taking them trick-or-treating with Safi. That weekend, we were scheduled to meet up with friends in Ohio. It felt like there was going to be a tiny break on the horizon from the dark clouds we'd been under since Soraya's birth.

This appointment started out like all the rest: medical history, height check, weight check. The nurse taking the inventory was a warm, motherly figure. I could tell she was experienced at her job, and I appreciated both her confidence and sensitivity toward the worried mom and tiny baby in front of her.

A medical student came in next, which the nurse had given me a heads-up about, and I'd consented. I thought, *This is totally fine. I believe in the process of teaching.* As he went through his spiel, I was half listening, half just biding my time until I got to see the doctor. Before that could happen, though, he dropped a total bomb on me. "So, how do you feel about getting a G tube?"

A G tube is a surgically implanted tube that runs from the abdomen into the stomach. A rubbery valve (think of the kind on a beach ball) provides access to the tube. When it's time for a feeding, the valve is opened, and one end of an external tube gets attached to the G tube while the other end is connected to a syringe containing liquid nutrition. The fluid then gets pushed out of the syringe, through the external tube, into the G tube, and then enters the stomach.

While there are no hard-and-fast rules about how to convey medical information to patients and their families, I personally believe a medical student should never be the one to bring up a potential surgery. If I were the doctor in charge, I would have told the student to get a good diet history and then ask what the family's expectations were in terms of moving forward. Some people may have already realized a G tube was inevitable, whereas others may have never even thought of it as a possibility. I was definitely in the latter camp, but the GI doctor clearly thought this was not going to be new information, so he allowed his medical student to handle the question—and now I was in shock.

My heart started hammering against my shirt. We hadn't even talked about supplementing with higher-calorie foods yet, and this student was suggesting carving a hole into my baby's belly to feed her! I was so angry, I was sweating. "I need to talk to the doctor," I declared.

The doctor came in and cut right to the chase. He was very kind, but his message was that Soraya was so far off the growth chart that a G tube was an absolute necessity. There was no other option.

"In the interim, we can get her in for a nasogastric [NG] tube on Monday," he continued as I stared at him dumbfounded. He was suggesting inserting a tube that runs through the nose and down into the stomach as a temporary way of getting more calories into Soraya.

"That way, you can start her on NG feeds while we prepare for the G tube placement."

I'm not sure how the doctor expected me to agree to schedule a surgery I hadn't even known was necessary until a few minutes ago, but it was not happening. I started sobbing to the point of hyperventilation. "Just give me a second," I said, gulping.

"Look, your baby needs to get this G tube," the doctor continued, trying to reason with me. "And before that gets placed, we need to look at her upper GI tract to check for reflux and you need to try to get her to gain some weight through an NG tube. You have to commit now if you want to get this all done by the time your husband is deployed in January."

They say humans react to stressful and frightening situations in one of three ways: fight, flight, or freeze. Well, I froze. I heard what he was saying. I understood the time constraints. But I was done. "I'll call you on Monday" was the most I could give him.

He left the room while the sweet, motherly nurse stayed behind. She pulled me into a warm hug. "I just need to talk to my husband," I said, crying into her shoulder.

"Don't worry," she told me. "I'll get you in whenever you're ready. I do all the scheduling."

I bawled the entire car ride home. I wasn't expecting to see Safi until it was time to take the girls trick-or-treating. Since there was no way I was telling him this latest bad news over the phone, I was just going to have to suck it up until then. I got Yasmeen into her fairy costume and Soraya into her baby elephant costume and took a slew of photos. I admired how sweet and adorable my girls looked, marveling at how no one would have any idea about the tough times our family was experiencing by looking at the pictures.

When Safi arrived home, I pulled him aside and got right to the point. It's one of those moments that will forever be seared into my brain. "You don't get to cry right now," I told him. "You have to take

Yasmeen trick-or-treating, because I can't do it. I'm going to sit here with Soraya. She doesn't know any different."

By now, we were used to taking turns holding each other up while the other one broke down. Right now was Safi's turn to fake a smile while I lost it, so he took Yasmeen for a little lap around the neighborhood and somehow managed to keep it together for her. Once they were back at home, we put her to bed and then just stared at each other, not even knowing where to start.

"Are we really okay to go to Ohio tomorrow?" I finally asked Safi.

"I don't think so," he said, looking hurt and bewildered.

I'd already given my sister—who was not only my "person" but also a psychologist—the play-by-play on the drive home from the appointment, and she'd told me in no uncertain terms that I was not to go anywhere at the moment. "Tasha, you're not in a good place," she'd said. "You just need to pause and be sad. That's the only thing you should be doing right now."

It was great advice, but I still wasn't quite ready to accept it. "What about my friends? They have all sorts of things planned for us!" I'd protested.

"They'll understand," she'd replied. "It's fine."

I knew my sister and Safi were right, so I started unpacking our already half-packed suitcases. As I put our clothes back into the drawers they came from, I mourned the life I thought we'd be living by now. The healthy baby I'd expected and hadn't been given. Trips to visit friends I thought I'd be able to enjoy. The grief from my ever-growing collection of losses washed over me in waves.

The next morning, I called in to work and took a mental health day. I spent it being sad, just like my sister advised. I held Soraya and hugged her, my tears falling onto her sweet head like a baptism of love and sorrow.

Friends called all day to offer support and encouragement. One gave me a pep talk that was particularly memorable. "Just get the tube in and get the food in as fast as you can," he urged. "Pump her up with those calories, wean off the tube, and then everything goes back to normal."

I felt my spirits lifting and my attitude about the G tube shifting. If Soraya wasn't meeting her milestones simply because she was malnourished, getting the G tube meant there was hope. I contacted the nurse and scheduled Soraya's appointments, feeling more optimistic than I had in months.

I truly believed this might be the answer and the end of a very long and difficult road—from Soraya's joyless birth to her first feeding when I videoed her stridor, to the swallow study where we found out she was aspirating, to the potential diagnosis of spinal muscular atrophy—and the beginning of a fresh new chapter. I hung on to the neurologist's assessment of Soraya's bright eyes and the thought that the G tube would solve everything.

I was determined to take back control of my out-of-control life. I wanted to find the source of Soraya's difficulties and fix whatever it was. I made a vow to myself: I was going to feed my baby until she was healthy, and everything would be smooth sailing from there on out.

Personal insight: I was *not* ready to receive any major information from the medical student. However, I likely wasn't ready to receive that information from the doctor either. I clung onto any bit of hope to keep me going, and for this part of my life it was primarily about giving calories to improve Soraya's condition.

Universal takeaway: When it comes to doctor's appointments, try not to have any expectations on outcomes. Come prepared with questions, and communicate that you need time to process any new information. It's also okay to be shattered from the information received and use hope to fuel your next best step.

Chapter 13

Fix You

Our attempt at a temporary salvation for getting more calories into Soraya—the nasogastric (NG) tube—was a total bust. She ripped the tubing out of her nose the first night it was in place, despite the heavy taping job Safi and I did. This behavior tracks for her: Soraya has strong opinions about what she will and will not do, not to mention sensory issues that complicate her ability to deal with external discomforts. Score: NG tube 0, Soraya 1.

Our team of doctors felt it was too risky to continue with the NG tube because removing it—which Soraya had already proven she was not only capable of—mid-feed could send liquid directly into her lungs. Since there was no other interim solution to increase her caloric intake, her G tube surgery was moved up to early December. This new date gave us a full month of training on the care and logistics of a G tube before Safi was scheduled to leave for Afghanistan. Having more of a buffer between his departure and the intense learning curve we were facing was a big relief.

Until then, we still had many, many tests and appointments to attend. At one of them, the neurologist and a rehab doctor confirmed our belief in the possibility that once Soraya was full of calories, her other difficulties might prove to be an aberration. Curing her malnutrition could potentially give her more strength, better tone, and put her back into typical ranges for height, weight, and milestones. I loved this idea, clinging to it like a life preserver.

The ear, nose, and throat specialist thought the issue might be an abnormal opening in Soraya's larynx called a *laryngeal cleft*. This is a rare condition where the esophagus (food tube) and trachea (breathing tube) are connected where they shouldn't be, allowing food and liquids to go into the lungs. I considered this option the second-best outcome, because Soraya could then have a surgery to correct the problem and she'd be good as new.

On the other end of the spectrum, though, there were still objectively awful and terrifying terminal diseases among the tests Soraya was undergoing. Safi and I got into a cycle of vacillating between buoyant hope and the depths of despair. Each of us spent countless hours every night researching all the possibilities that had been discussed, looking for "the" answer or trying to discover something new the doctors hadn't yet considered. It was unimaginably exhausting, but the prospect of finding the missing piece of the puzzle was too tantalizing to ignore.

What ifs swirled around us like a tornado. What if it was nothing? What if it was the worst thing possible? What if Soraya turned out to be completely fine? What if she never made it past her first birthday?

In our minds, the dichotomy of her condition either being something fixable or something terminal played on a never-ending loop. There was never any in-between. The choices were (1) death or (2) we're going to fix it and she's going to catch up.

And, as if things couldn't be more complicated than they already were, Safi was scheduled to have a vasectomy, which we'd decided to go forward with as planned as soon as Soraya was born. The military recommends families wait until their youngest child is six months old before having the procedure, and by now Soraya was almost seven months old. We already had the two children we'd agreed on, so it was time, and doing the vasectomy before Safi was deployed made perfect sense in our minds.

The geneticist and genetic counselor we were working with quickly threw a wrench in that plan. "How many children are you planning to have?" they asked us.

I bristled. The question seemed overly personal, bordering on invasive. "Two. And we already have them."

"Okay, now let me ask you this," the genetic counselor continued. "*Why* did you decide on two children?"

Safi and I looked at each other. He cleared his throat. I took a deep breath. "We didn't want to have an only child," I admitted.

The follow-up question to that hung in the air, unspoken, even before words were put to it. "So, what are you going to do if one dies?"

Safi and I looked at each other, completely aghast. Neither of us had language to fill the space where such a painful potential reality had been uttered out loud. I realize now the genetic counselor had most certainly dealt with this reaction before—the shock, the anger, the horror—and asking those questions was part of their job. At the time, though, it felt like a slap in the face. Another injustice in a vast and growing series of them.

"Wait. What?" I couldn't even fathom having an answer.

"Would you have another baby?" the genetic counselor persisted.

Safi—who my dear cousin Julie sometimes refers to as a "spicy meatball" due to his indomitable fiery streak—was livid. "Oh, so you think we can just replace Soraya? What kind of question is that?!"

Recognizing our high emotional state, discomfort, and lack of clarity, the geneticist recommended putting the vasectomy off at least until Soraya's testing was complete because the results might affect our decision about having more kids. As taken aback as we were, we understood the logic behind gathering all the pertinent information and pausing to reflect before doing something not easily reversed. We agreed to wait.

By now, Soraya's surgery was fast approaching. The plan was to admit Soraya to the hospital for a full two weeks, which would make juggling our full-time jobs and Yasmeen tough. I took a week off from work so I could be with Soraya for the initial part of her recovery. Safi was using vacation days to handle the second weeklong shift. My mom and Safi's mom were each coming for a week to help with a bit of everything—learning to do the G tube feeds along with us, watching Soraya in the hospital when we needed to step away for a moment, and keeping Yasmeen occupied before and after daycare when Safi and I weren't there.

Three-and-a-half year-old Yasmeen was now a full participant in the chaos our lives had become. She'd always been bright, curious, compliant, and adaptable—really, she was the overachiever of kids—so I truly believed in my heart that she would come out of all this relatively unscathed. Terrible as it may sound, I almost felt like her adaptability gave me license to pour everything I had into finding a cure for Soraya and not give nearly as much of myself to Yasmeen as I should have.

My thinking at the time went something like this: *Yasmeen is healthy. She has clothes on her body, a roof over her head, and two parents who love her, albeit rather distractedly as of late. What does she have to be upset about? Nothing.*

I know exactly where this "suck it up, buttercup" attitude originated. I learned it from the best of the best: my mom. Whenever I got a bad grade, had an issue with a friend, or was sad about something, she never failed to remind me that other people had it way worse than I did, so I might as well stop wallowing and start moving forward. At best it was an okay approach under minor circumstances, but during a prolonged hardship with no end in sight, it wasn't helpful—especially when applied to a toddler.

Before Soraya was born, we were happy, upbeat, and totally focused on Yasmeen, and now she was running a very distant second to her sick little sister. *Of course* she was feeling the effects of that. To give myself a little grace, I truly was at my limit, but it still makes me want to cry just thinking about it.

On the appointed day, we checked into the hospital. Soraya successfully had the G tube placed, got ear tubes, and endured a spinal tap all in the same surgery. We decided to multitask so we could minimize the amount of anesthesia she had to be under.

As soon as the surgery was over, the doctors informed us they hadn't found a laryngeal cleft. It was a disappointment to have to cross that one out as a possibility. As a result, we hung even more hope on the idea that this was simply a case of malnutrition.

Every morning in the hospital, Soraya got a schedule detailing the specific therapies she would have that day. Speech therapy worked with her on oral feedings. Physical therapy focused on her gross motor skills. Occupational therapy looked to improve her fine motor skills as well as her trunk and core strength. It was like a jam-packed summer camp itinerary; only less fun and more imperative she give her all at every event.

As Soraya's G tube feeds increased, so did her weight. She made strides at taking a bottle. She drank more in one sitting than she ever had before—a few ounces in a single feeding! We'd never seen her pee so much. When she swallowed water and it didn't go into her lungs, it felt like a miracle.

Yasmeen came to the hospital to visit her little sister exactly once. Although we thought it was a great idea at the time, we now know it was a mistake. What small child would be able to process all those tubes and a hole in her sister's stomach without developing at least a little post-traumatic stress disorder? Dressed as Sleeping Beauty, she read Soraya a story, offered her a cookie, and then asked to not come back again.

To make up for taking Yasmeen away from her regular routine, we showered her with a little extra attention after that. Safi took her to see a Disney Live show. We both treated her with a visit to a train museum while the grandmothers stayed with Soraya. We figured things had evened out a bit after that.

97

Fix You

By the time we were discharged, the doctors were very impressed with Soraya's progress. We knew we still had a long road ahead of us, but we had so much hope that things were finally on the right track. Once Soraya gained enough weight, we could get back to the life we were meant to be living.

Personal insight: How I wish I could go back in time and focus more on Yasmeen. I had tunnel vision to save Soraya and I had faith in myself that I could shift my attention as soon as Soraya was on track. I never imagined that getting her on track would never really happen. If I could go back in time, I would be proactive in Yasmeen's life versus waiting for signs of anxiety and then responding.

Universal takeaway: Siblings of children with any medical needs need dedicated time and attention from their parents or caregivers. Just because children are known to be resilient doesn't mean they should be left to parent themselves. The impact of how you parent your children in those critical moments (and honestly in the daily routine as well) have lasting effects.

Chapter 14

Underwater

All that optimism dissipated once we got home. As we were unpacking the myriad supplies that go along with a G tube, it quickly became apparent that we were going to have to reorganize the kitchen. There were miles of tubing, piles of syringes, cases of formula, and boxes of medications—to name a few. We needed more cabinet space, more drawers. We had to go out and buy an extra fridge and bottle warmer for our bedroom so we could prepare Soraya's feeds without interrupting her sleep.

Worse, what had seemed relatively straightforward in the hospital was more complicated once we were at home along with her. The medical company failed to deliver Soraya's formula as scheduled, so an exhausted Safi had to head back out to the hospital and get enough samples to tide us over until our supply arrived. Once he was back home, we realized no one had ever told us how to prepare it for the increased calories she was now prescribed. Even as two trained physicians, we fumbled.

What's more, Soraya's nutrition schedule was hectic and relentless. There were six nonnegotiable feeding times: 9:00 a.m., 1:00 p.m., 5:00 p.m., 9:00 p.m., 1:00 a.m., 5:00 a.m. Never mind if Soraya was resting, sleeping, happily content, playing, or not hungry at the allotted times.

Each feeding started with warming a bottle—Soraya would only take it if it was warm—and then offering it to her. Once she was done drinking on her own (which usually happened after an ounce or two), we moved on to putting the rest of the amount in a syringe and slowly pushing it into her G tube. Because of her reflux, she would often vomit during one of these steps. When that happened, we'd have to estimate what had been rejected, put this amount into the syringe, and push it into the G tube.

Each feeding took over an hour. Even after it was over we had to stick around to make sure Soraya didn't vomit again. If she did, the amount that came up needed to go right back in. I couldn't fathom how we were ever going to be able to care for Soraya, parent Yasmeen, go to work, and get any sleep again.

To top it all off, the first thing Yasmeen said when we got home from the hospital was "I want a Christmas tree."

Safi and I had always intended to raise our children with the Islamic faith, since we are both Muslims. We'd negotiated a compromise that would provide them with a more structured religious education than I was raised with but one that was less strict than Safi's had been. Even though I was totally on board with that plan at the time, I remember commenting that I thought giving up Christmas—which my family had always celebrated in a nonreligious way—was going to be tough for me.

"I understand, but that's what I had to do," Safi told me. "I want the girls to feel proud of who they are."

But now that our lives had been turned completely upside down, denying our toddler's request for a nonreligious Christmas tree wasn't a battle we wanted to fight. We went out, got a tree, and didn't care what anyone thought or said about it. It clearly meant our house had been turned into a medical supply store overnight, and this tree was the only happy thing in it.

Yet as excited as Yasmeen was about having "Christmas," it became obvious she was now struggling right along with us. She was curious about the G tube but annoyed that Soraya's new feeding schedule interfered with her normal daily routine. Soraya was gaining weight, which led to a much more vigorous cry—which of course woke Yasmeen up nightly, making our usually well-adjusted older child cranky and irritable. All this meant I was under more pressure to "fix" everything, and I had fewer answers than ever as to how I was going to accomplish such a momentous feat.

As the reality settled in of what our daily life was going to look like for the foreseeable future, I was finally forced to admit that something had to give. Although I was still required to work full-time to fulfill my commitment to the National Health Service Corps, I was able to negotiate two mornings off every week in exchange for working two nights. Even though my clinic had never offered evening hours before, it was a beneficial adjustment because the timing was more convenient for many patients. As for me, I knew I'd be getting less sleep than ever, but at least I'd be able to take Soraya to many of her six weekly therapy sessions and multitude of additional doctor appointments.

At home, the only way to keep up with the new routine at home was to divide and conquer. Safi agreed to cover Soraya's 1:00 a.m. feed while I took on the 9:00 p.m. and five a.m. shifts because I didn't mind getting up early. My little secret was that during every 9:00 p.m. feed, I'd sit and sob. I used the time to talk to God, and it was less a prayer of *Please help my child* and more one of *Please help me. I can't do this. I'm not strong enough.* People love to say God doesn't give you anything you can't handle, but at that moment, I was like *I can't handle this. I really can't.* On the worst nights, my thoughts went to some very dark places, such as *Either I need to die or she does, because I can't keep going like this.*

Even on top of Soraya's extraordinary nutritional needs, she was also frequently sick with ear infections, pneumonia, and the symptoms of reflux. It was a constant battle to get her to settle down and fall asleep. I'm sure it's not comfortable being pumped full of milk before bed, but there was no other option. It was a never-ending merry-go-round of pain and misery.

One night I was at my wit's end. I could not get Soraya—or myself—to stop crying. I'd tried every trick in the book, and she was having none of it. Being unable to calm my own child left me feeling so helpless and like such a failure, I just had to tap out and take a moment.

I texted Safi, *I know it's my turn, but I can't do it.* He came into the room, tried to settle Soraya unsuccessfully for several minutes, and then put her down. He came out of her room and told me, "I need a break, too."

We left her room and sat at the kitchen table. Soraya was still screaming. "I don't know how we're going to do this," I whispered to Safi. "And I especially don't know how I'm going to do it alone once you're deployed."

"Shhhh," he said, pointing at the video baby monitor we had set up in Soraya's room. "Look!"

I stared into the monitor and watched as a white ball of light seemed to stroke Soraya until she calmed down enough to go to sleep. Safi and I looked at each other in disbelief. There seemed no other explanation than God knew I was at my breaking point, heard my prayers, and sent an angel to soothe Soraya's pain. To this day, it's still the only explanation I can conjure up.

And in that moment, something shifted. Whether it was simply acceptance that this was our fate or the revelation that angels were helping us care for our desperately ill child, I felt a sudden surge of strength welling up inside of me. I started giving Safi the pep talk that I probably needed far more than he did.

"We need to realize this is our life now," I declared. "This is just the way it's going to be. We're in survival mode, so we have to buckle in and get on with it. No more complaining about how tired we are. If we need more caffeine, we'll drink more caffeine. We're doing this so Soraya can live."

For whatever reason, it worked for us both. After that, we didn't talk about how hard our lives were anymore. We knew the constant airing of complaints, questioning why this was happening to us, and comparing ourselves to other people wasn't healthy. We knew we had to change.

As Dear Sugar (AKA Cheryl Strayed, author of *Wild*) once noted in the book *Tiny Beautiful Things*, "Most things will be okay eventually, but not everything will be. Sometimes you'll put up a good fight and lose. Sometimes you'll hold on really hard and realize there is no choice but to let go. Acceptance is a small, quiet room."

The realization that we were just going to have to live in this small, quiet room until we found the key out of there settled in.

Personal insight: The nights I would sob while rocking Soraya I finally realized that I had two choices. I could either sink into a deeper, darker depression or I could shift my perspective. I realized there was nothing else I could change.

Universal take away: There are times that you will feel like you are drowning. You can succumb to that despair or you can push through with a mind shift. There will be times when the only thing you can change is your perspective.

Chapter 15

All I Need

My biggest goal became getting the G tube out as fast as possible. I was willing to do almost anything to achieve this goal. The doctors told us Soraya would need to consistently take 90% of her calories by mouth for that to happen, so that became my main focus.

Our kitchen became a veritable war zone where the enemy was resorting to using the G tube. To distract Soraya enough to get her to take her food by mouth, we'd turn on the TV during these very tense and unpleasant "meals"—a pediatrician no-no if there ever was one. We recruited Yasmeen to blow bubbles and sing songs to her sister. Alternately, we urged her to keep her mouth shut and not say a word when we didn't want Soraya distracted. She was very obedient but sometimes forgot and said or did something we thought might alter our success that night. That never failed to earn her a reprimand of *We're almost through the bottle; be quiet!*

Culturally, Safi and I were both raised with the idea that the oldest child needs to take responsibility for the younger kids in a family. This duty is just ingrained in us. Remember, my dad took over financial responsibility for his *10* siblings and their children after his father died! The minute we knew a baby was coming, our message to Yasmeen had been *You're going to be our little helper.* Once Soraya was born and we found out she had special needs, it was *Yasmeen, you're the eldest. If something ever happens to us, you will have to take care of Soraya for the rest of her life.* Yes, these words were spoken out loud to our four-year-old. At the time, I believed this was a critical piece of our culture, but now I have many regrets about putting this kind of pressure on a small child.

Whenever I could, I'd also bring Yasmeen with me to Soraya's therapies to spend more quality time with her. On our better days, she seemed to enjoy it at least a little bit. But then as we were driving home from yet another session, Yasmeen piped up from the back seat, "You might as well throw me out now. You don't need me."

I was stunned into silence. I'm sure I tried to reassure Yasmeen that I did, in fact, love her and need her wholeheartedly. But she looked not only skeptical but also miserable in response. The words that had come out of my obviously hurt and resentful child were devastating and unforgettable. Safi and I got her into therapy immediately.

My sister, the psychologist, was forever suggesting that I learn to take care of myself as well. She kept saying things like "You need time for self-care." I always thought, *Yeah, when? How?* I really couldn't figure out a way to fit that in—but I also realized that how I was currently doing things was no longer working.

She tried her best to normalize asking for help: I was in a chronic stressful situation, and just getting through it wasn't an option anymore. When I failed to respond to that, she finally stopped beating around the bush. "It's probably a good idea for you and Safi to get into therapy, too."

I was like, "Whoa, whoa, whoa! We're doing just fine."

But I wasn't. She knew it and I knew it. I gave in, called a therapist who looked promising, and met them in person for a consultation to see if we'd be a good fit. I explained my anxiety about not having time to do therapy and they promised to work around my schedule. They even suggested bringing Soraya with me to appointments to decrease the stress of having to find a babysitter. I was like, *Alright, I'm finally doing this. These people seem fabulous. I'm finally going to start taking care of myself, and I can bring Soraya!*

106

Keep Your Head Up

At our very first appointment, though, the therapist didn't show up. In fact, the entire office was closed. I called the emergency number multiple times, but my messages went unreturned. I had brought everything I needed to feed Soraya with me: a bottle warmer, formula, syringes, tubing.

I'd already explained to this potential therapist that a little piece of me crumbled every time I attached the tubing to Soraya's G tube. All I could think was *I can't believe I'm doing this. I can't believe this is how she has to eat.* Whenever I had to feed Soraya in public, I felt like everyone was staring at us and feeling sorry for us. It didn't help that I ended up crying every time, which made me hate the G tube—and myself—even more. And now here I was, with no way to warm up the bottle and feeding her through a G tube in the trunk of my car. In my mind, it was inexcusable that I had been put in this position.

Finally, the therapist called me back and said she'd been stuck in an emergency. I thought, *You're a therapist, I shouldn't have to tell you establishing trust is the foundation of any good relationship.* I'd told this person how hard it was going to be for me to even be there and they weren't meeting me where I was at. My perspective at that time was literal survival. Every day was a Groundhog Day of another test, another inconclusive result. There was absolutely no end in sight. Looking back, I realize I had zero reserve. I was running on empty. I needed the therapist to help me to get to even half a gallon, but that hadn't happened.

After that experience, finding a new therapist felt like just another stressor in my life. I kept thinking, *What if that person doesn't show up? I can't risk it.* It's not usually like me to give up after one try, but I had poured everything I had into getting to that first visit. I was not about to give another therapist another chance to leave me and my child high and dry.

So, there would be no therapy anytime soon. There was zero time in my nonstop schedule for self-care. I was lucky to be able to grab a few hours of sleep and a shower every day. I was just going to have to keep on keeping on. I had no idea how I was going to pull it off. I only knew that I had to.

And there was still more scrambling that needed to be done before then. The daycare Soraya and Yasmeen attended and loved so much let us know they would not be able to manage Soraya's regimented feeding schedule. They simply weren't staffed to handle a baby with a G tube, especially one with so many feeds that took so long. This left us in a quandary. Who could we trust to care for and feed Soraya while we were at work, especially given the nightmare experience we'd had with the swing-kicking nanny?

In a Hail Mary pass, I reached out to an occasional date night sitter we'd had a great experience with and asked if she might consider rearranging her grad school schedule to accommodate working for us. She quickly said yes, agreeing to not only learn how to use the G tube but also to accompany Soraya to her therapies on the days I was working. I considered her just as much of an angel as the white light that had comforted Soraya during our darkest hour.

Working full-time along with six hours of therapy a week, plus daily "homework" was a lot. I was already having a hard enough time covering two half days of therapies a week, and I was now lucky enough to have a babysitter helping me on the other days. As a doctor, it had never occurred to me what parents had to do when I ordered these types of interventions.

During the first several months of juggling Soraya's therapy schedule, I was baffled. I remember asking the therapists, "Do people just take off work to come to therapy? Or do they have to quit work?" Not that quitting or scaling back to a part-time schedule was even a possibility because I still needed to fulfill my commitment to the NHSC. I was just going to have to find a way to do it all.

Feeding therapy was the bane of my existence. The progress was painfully, painfully slow. The goal was to have Soraya drinking from a

108

Keep Your Head Up

bottle, eating food, and swallowing correctly. If she could do that, we'd get her off the tube feeds—my biggest hope at the time. The therapists would have her finger paint with applesauce, or rub it on her face, or kiss it. It was torturous to see her only take a single bite after all that.

Next, there was physical therapy. The goal was to increase Soraya's core strength. They worked on getting her to sit up on her own, something she hadn't quite managed yet—she'd often topple over and didn't have the muscular ability to write herself. They also tried to get her to crawl by placing her on all fours, but she had a hard time supporting weight on her hands. She liked being placed on her feet but could not pull to stand on her own. While this was still a glacial process, it was far less excruciating than feeding therapy.

The third modality was speech therapy, which focused on getting Soraya to vocalize more. She shone the brightest here, displaying improvements much more quickly than in feeding or physical therapies. She started saying Mama and Dada (nonspecifically, more like babbling, but still), and the sound of her little voice emerging thrilled me.

As Safi's deployment drew nearer, it started to feel like the weight of the world was about to crush me. Sure, I'd talked some big talk about how I'd be able to handle it all on my own. Now as reality was sinking in, I was beginning to doubt any human being could do everything that needed to be done on their own, babysitter or no babysitter. I knew I'd simply have to manage Soraya's care, parenting both girls, and my work schedule without Safi's help, but there was never a part of me that felt like *I got this*. It truly seemed like an impossible task.

All I could think was that Safi was either going to miss Soraya's first step, or he was going to miss her death—and either way, he was going to be missing something big. Those two outcomes were still the only options I could fathom. However, I knew a commitment was a commitment, especially when it came to the military.

"Did you hear anything today?" I asked Safi when he got home from work every day.

The answer was always no, until one day he said something I never in a million years dreamed could happen. "Rob's going to take it for me," he announced.

Safi had met his medical partners, Rob Ruland and Chris Hogan, in the navy. Since both were more seasoned in the military, they had taken Safi under their wing. Now Rob, who was a higher rank than Safi, had taken it on himself to ask if he could go to Afghanistan in Safi's place. This kind of swap is unheard of, but because it was a hand surgeon for a hand surgeon, the request was approved. This was made even more unbelievable because Rob had already done his time, wasn't up to be deployed again, and still had a high school–aged son at home. In his mind, though, we had a sick baby to take care of, and he wanted Safi to be there for Soraya.

I gasped. "That's not possible. Is it?"

Safi nodded, tears running down his cheeks.

"Are you sure?" I whispered. As much as I didn't want Rob to be deployed in Safi's place, I was beyond relieved and grateful for his incredibly generous gesture.

"It's already done and approved. I can stay."

It was just another miracle, like the white light that comforted Soraya when both of us were unable to soothe her. There will never be enough words of gratitude to thank Rob for giving such a beautiful gift to our family. He truly brought us to our knees with his goodness and self-sacrifice, which meant everything to us.

Now, much to our relief, there would be no deployment. I would not have to go it alone. Both Soraya and Yasmeen would have two parents helping them weather this storm. As a minuscule token of my appreciation—though nothing can ever repay this beautiful man for sacrificing himself for our family—I offered to have his son, who wanted to attend medical school someday, shadow me while he was away. The son often talked about missing his dad, who was now in Afghanistan in Safi's place, as we were seeing patients in the clinic together. I invited him over many times so he could get to know Soraya and learn about her medical needs. I wanted him to understand who and what his dad was doing this for, why it mattered so much to us, and how grateful we were to him.

Then, as it still is today, I found it incredibly hard to accept help, knowing there was no way I could reciprocate these grand gestures or even the multitude of small, kind favors we'd been given. Learning to receive has been an equally difficult and beautiful lesson for me, and I just keep trying to do so with grace and gratitude, and minus all the guilt.

Like everyone, I'm still a work in progress.

Personal insight: Safi's friend Rob took his deployment. This is the greatest and most unexpected act of friendship. We had been trying so hard to repay this act of service to Rob and his family. There will be nothing we can do that compares to that. Not being able to return favors have oftentimes made it difficult for me to *accept* favors. However, being free of Safi's deployment forced me to look at this in a different way.

Universal take away: Sometimes people show up for you in the most unexpected ways. Not every good deed is meant to be reciprocated, *and* there's no tally system in life for paybacks. What you can't pay back, pay forward and do so without expecting anything in return.

Chapter 16

Vindicated

By this point, Soraya was fast approaching her first birthday. Although she'd made some great progress, she most certainly wasn't meeting those baby milestones within the conventional time frame. She wasn't talking. She wasn't walking. She still wasn't eating much by mouth.

"I want a sister or brother who can dance with me," Yasmeen told us on repeat. "I want one who can eat with me. Won't you please have another baby?"

She was only four years old at the time, but I took her request seriously. I recognized that we had done everything as a family to help Soraya without taking into consideration the impact it might have on Yasmeen. I also understood her desire for a more neurotypical sibling was not likely to go away no matter how old she got.

Besides, the nagging questions the geneticist had posed to us were still lingering out there in the ether: *Why did you decide to have two children? Oh, you didn't want to have an only child? Well, what are you going to do if one dies?* The one thing Safi and I knew for sure was that we did not want to have an only child. We had both been very close to our siblings growing up and wanted our children to have that same opportunity.

I broached the subject with Safi one night after we'd put Yasmeen to bed and in between Soraya's feedings. I considered it a minor miracle that we were both awake at the same time. Chronic sleep deprivation was our new normal.

"What do you think about having another baby? I don't think it's fair for Yasmeen to have the sole burden of caring for Soraya if something happens to us," I said.

Safi was silent for a moment, seemingly considering the possibility. Then he blurted out, "What if the third one's a complete disaster?"

I started laughing so hard I could barely get any words out. "I honestly don't think we need to be concerned about that."

Despite the moment of humor, Yasmeen's yearning for a more typical sibling opened some painful but very honest discussions between us. We talked about what it would look like for Yasmeen to have sole responsibility for Soraya if we were no longer around. We knew now we didn't want Yasmeen's whole life to be shaped by taking care of her sister, which was exactly what we'd been grooming her for and, on further consideration, not at all what we wanted for her.

The other side of the coin held an equally difficult moral question: was having another child just to help out Yasmeen a justifiable reason to do so? Yes, it would take the pressure off our eldest—but what if that potential future child didn't *want* to share in that responsibility? Or what if they also had special needs? There was nothing we'd uncovered to lead us to believe that would happen, but it was always a possibility and neither of us thought we could handle that. The questions were enough to spin our minds into a frenzy.

Ultimately, we decided to put the final decision on hold while we pushed for every genetic test available, not only to help us solidify whether having another child was in the cards for us but also as part of our never-ending quest to "fix" whatever was wrong with Soraya by leaving no stone unturned. We knew there was a muscle biopsy that could tell us if she had mitochondrial disease or any muscular dystrophies. We'd also heard about an exome study that could determine if a recessive gene was responsible for Soraya's difficulties (and we knew that if there was a genetic component, it could not be dominant or Yasmeen would have had it, too). And, as our genetics team had warned us, there was the possibility we could do every test in existence and *still* never know what was causing her symptoms.

We decided to forge ahead with the testing. Maybe we'd find out Soraya had a treatable condition, and this whole nightmare would end. We'd likely determine if having another child was a risk we were willing to take because if a muscle biopsy came back negative like all the other tests had, science would have proven to us there was no genetic reason to believe we'd have another special needs child. We felt both outcomes were worth the time and effort.

Since the muscle biopsy was a specialized test, costing $50,000, and Rainbow Babies in Cleveland was only one of two hospitals doing it at the time, there were no guarantees it would even be an option for us. The military typically does not offer the most generous benefits when it comes to genetic tests, and this was expensive, advanced medical technology. We submitted the procedure for insurance precertification and held our collective breath.

Insurance denied our first request quickly. We gathered letters of support from our geneticist and the lab director and submitted an appeal. Preapproval was necessary before we could schedule anything, so there was nothing to do now but wait.

In the interim, we continued with our new normal: physical, speech, feeding, and occupational therapies, twice a week for each modality. We had Soraya fitted for shoe inserts to help stabilize her feet. We had her assessed for both standers and gait trainers that would help her bear weight, stimulate bone growth, and encourage mobility. We got her special clothes for sensory input and to help support her low muscle tone. Basically, we were throwing everything we could at maximizing her abilities, whatever they turned out to be.

Those always seemed to follow a progression and plateau cycle. Soraya would seemingly gain a skill, then somehow lose it for several weeks or even months, and then get it back again. To my pediatrician brain this made no sense, and I spent far too much time trying to piece together why it kept happening.

She added the words *bowl*, *bye-bye*, *two*, and *moo* to her vocabulary but still had a significant speech delay to overcome. In response, I conducted constant one-sided conversations with her all day long. *How was your day? Oh, it was good? What did you do?* I knew she could hear me and maybe understand some of the things I was saying. I would not give up.

Much to my chagrin, the G tube was still providing most of Soraya's nutrition. Whenever she tried to drink from a bottle, she'd start sweating and tire out quickly. Using a sippy cup garnered similarly poor results. She would only deign to drink from a straw if Yasmeen was doing it as well. There were several weeks where she seemed to be in horrible pain, was not sleeping well, and barely ate—presumably due to reflux, but who really knew anything for certain at this point—until finally, after an increase in meds and the tincture of time, she began taking in nutrition again.

And then, almost miraculously, Soraya began pulling up to stand, cruising, and crawling up the steps of our house. But then, just as suddenly, she was doing none of it at all again. *Is this a regression*, I wondered, *or is she just gathering energy for the next big surge?* Two long months later, she started trying to stand again but was nowhere near where she'd been before. As a pediatrician, this made no sense to me. Typically, once a child learns a skill, it is not only maintained but also continues to grow. Her acquisitions were unpredictable and all over the place.

Every day, Soraya had to spend an hour in the stander to force her to put weight on her legs, build bone density and muscle strength, and learn to walk. I could rarely bear to put her in it myself. Strapping her in—her feet in buckles, legs sealed into a backing, hips secured into a harness—felt barbaric to me, like I was affixing her to a torture device.

"Safi, I need you to put Soraya in her stander. I just can't," I told him time and again. "How do you not feel awful putting her in this?"

"Because her bones need this. Without it, her legs will never be able to support her," he'd tell me, his experience as an orthopedic surgeon and calm, practical demeanor easing my anxiety as always. "Remember, I've had many patients go through this, so I know it works."

There was an activity table attached to the stander, so we offered Soraya all her favorite toys to play with. We'd pop in a movie to keep her distracted; *The Little Mermaid* was her favorite. Despite these attempts, Soraya absolutely hated everything about this process—it was boring, and it was hard work. She was not participating on her own terms and motivating her to do something that was not her choice was as hard as it would be with any toddler. Progress was painfully slow and came only sporadically.

Mama Mary had recently advised me to think of Soraya's energy as being confined to a small pot. Whenever she got sick or tired, she needed to hibernate like a bear to restore it. While this explanation of her cycle of waxing and waning vitality rang true to me, it did nothing to calm my frantic and frenzied thoughts.

We still don't know what this is.

Whatever skills Soraya has gained could go away at any point.

How can we at least improve her quality of life if it turns out we can't "fix" whatever this is?

WHAT THE HELL DOES SHE HAVE???

I tried to shut down the terrified voice in my head, but fear has a way of amplifying our worst imaginings. I held on tightly to our doctor's words to comfort myself: *Soraya continues to progress and there's no data that tells us this will change in the future.*

While we were busy throwing ourselves into Soraya's therapy "homework," we received yet another denial from the insurance company. As frustrating as that was, we also recognized how much they had already covered for Soraya. Still, our gratitude didn't relieve the agony of not knowing what was causing her medical problems. We decided that even if this next and final appeal garnered a no, we would find an alternate way to cover the $50,000 bill for the testing. It was that important to us.

Knowing how important this last appeal was, Safi wrote to members of Congress, pleading our case. He let them know this study was the only option left that might be able to provide a diagnosis, prognosis, and more effective treatments for our little girl. That's not to say we were giving up or losing hope yet. In fact, we were doing anything and everything we could to get them to say yes.

In talking to the insurance company, we learned that having the geneticist at Rainbow Babies examine Soraya and weigh in about their findings might swing the case in our favor. With a strict time limit to get the appeal submitted and the clock ticking, we added a visit to Cleveland to our already full to-do list. Since my brother's upcoming wedding was being held in Detroit, which is relatively close to Cleveland, of course we decided to fit both events into a single weekend. We're nothing if not overachievers.

We flew into Detroit as a family the night before the appointment. A dear friend of mine, who lives in Toledo and is a genetic counselor, met me there leaving her own family to help mine out. She took a quick nap at the hotel before waking up at four in the morning to drive me and Soraya to Cleveland. Safi and Yasmeen stayed behind to enjoy the pre-wedding festivities.

At the evaluation, I went through Soraya's entire complicated history with the geneticist and asked if the muscle biopsy could potentially be useful in diagnosing and treating her. The doctor was cautiously optimistic and encouraging about the procedure. We then met with the doctor who would do the surgery if it were approved (or when we figured out how to pay for it), and they seemed wonderful. I gathered the required paperwork for the final appeal and submitted it, sending it into the ether with a prayer for success.

My dear friend managed to return us back to Detroit in time for the rehearsal dinner. The next day, Yasmeen was a gorgeous, spunky flower girl at the wedding. Soraya got lots of love from her cousins, aunts, uncles, and grandparents and even went for a swim with Nana.

It almost felt like we were a regular family for a minute there.

Personal insight: I realized that we were so desperate to find answers for Soraya. The muscle biopsy to assess for mitochondrial disease was our last available testing that we hadn't done for Soraya. We were at an intersection of deciding to have another child, and we based our next step on the results from the muscle biopsy that insurance denied.

Universal takeaway: When it comes to insurance denials, you may feel frustrated, defeated, and helpless. Don't stay in that space. Get up and *rally*. Do everything you can to share your story and ask your medical team to help. Letters and calls to Congress *can* help.

Chapter 17

I Still Haven't Found
What I'm Looking For

Three weeks later, we received the exciting news that the insurance company had finally approved Soraya's muscle biopsy. Safi had single-handedly made this happen through his tireless advocacy. He'd consulted with Rainbow Babies multiple times to determine what further proof they needed, solicited letters of support from a variety of doctors, and, through a work connection, even contacted the Assistant Secretary of Defense of Health to ask for governmental backing. He did all the legwork and didn't give up until we got what we needed for Soraya. Additionally, the approval could potentially improve the way military insurance views other children in similar situations in the future, and we hoped our victory would pave the way for other families so they didn't have to face our same struggles.

We flew as a family from Virginia to Rainbow Babies for the procedure, and my mom traveled from South Bend to Cleveland to help us out wherever she was needed. All of us were buoyed by the hope that this procedure would provide the diagnosis and treatment path we'd been so desperately seeking. Although Soraya's wide range of symptoms had not fit any one disease completely, mitochondrial disease now seemed the most likely culprit. It was possible it wouldn't show up in blood tests but would appear in the muscle. And while there is no cure for mitochondrial disease, a positive result would at least enable us to consult the top experts in the field and give Soraya the best care available.

In our minds, the test held the potential to vastly improve the quality of Soraya's life. If it showed a positive result, we'd finally have a cause and cure to put all our efforts behind. Being undiagnosed has a way of making families feel even more isolated, unheard, and unseen than dealing with a chronically ill child already does, because there's no support group to join, specially colored ribbon to wear, or 5K to run with other people affected by the same disease.

Safi was very concerned Soraya would be left with a scar after the biopsy. As a surgeon himself, he prides himself on clean incisions and minimal scarring. Before the procedure, he questioned the surgeon about how large and long the incision would be.

"I have patients with scars that make it harder for them to feel confident and like how they look in the mirror," Safi explained. "So, I want to make sure this is done in the least invasive way possible." He was reassured they would take as little tissue as possible from Soraya's leg and work diligently to ensure the scarring was slight.

My mom watched Yasmeen in the hotel room while Safi and I were present at the muscle biopsy. The surgeon ended up taking a much larger chunk from Soraya's leg than we anticipated, and she was in a great deal of pain after the procedure. I'm sure the medical team only did what they had to do, but it was really hard on both of us to see Soraya suffer like that. We started questioning how far we were willing to go to get a diagnosis for her.

"What did we just do?" I asked when I saw our spunky Soraya wincing, whimpering, and desperate to be held. "Why did we put her through this?"

We flew back to Virginia awash in the knowledge that we'd chosen this path for her. Still, the result of this test would be our closure, no matter what it revealed. We wouldn't change our decision either then or now, but it was exceedingly hard to reconcile in the moment.

In fact, it made us start questioning everything we'd been running full force at since Soraya's birth. *How much suffering can one child be expected to endure? Are we even doing the right thing? At what point do we stop? Is uncovering every stone worth it? Maybe we should just let things be.*

We had been told the results of the muscle biopsy would take a while to come back, so Safi and I took advantage of my sister's offer to watch the girls and headed off on an adults-only weekend to Miami to talk more about the pros and cons of having another child. As the genetic counselor had explained, women 35 and older are considered to be of "advanced maternal age," so if I didn't become pregnant within the next several years, the odds of having a baby with a genetic anomaly would increase significantly. The pressure was on.

We volleyed around all sorts of questions while enjoying the warm weather in Miami. Were we going to have another baby? If yes, why? And what would our efforts look like? How far would we go to achieve our goal? Would we pursue fertility treatments if nature didn't do the trick?

Through all the back-and-forth—what if the third one is a complete disaster, what if they have a genetic deformity, what if we have to go through the trauma of aborting—what finally got both of us on the same page was Yasmeen. We were taking her word that she needed a sibling experience that Soraya could sadly not provide for her. Granted, that didn't mean we could necessarily make her wish come true, but we were willing to give it our best shot.

We made several promises to each other. First, Safi made me swear I wouldn't breastfeed—that was his top condition. He recognized that it had not been good for any of us, me most of all.

"It took so much of your energy," he explained. "You couldn't be present for yourself or Yasmeen. I really need you to agree to this for us and our family."

"You can't tell me that I can't breastfeed," I pushed back. I really wanted that skin-to-skin contact once the baby arrived. I also wanted to "succeed" at breastfeeding, just like everything else in life.

"Okay," he countered, gently but firmly adding in a stipulation. "But at the first sign things aren't going well—the baby's not gaining weight, gets sick, is not having wet diapers, or has any difficulty latching—I need you to stop for everyone's health and well-being, especially your own."

"Fine," I agreed, hanging on to hope that no problems would appear, and I'd get to enjoy this aspect of motherhood the way I wanted to this time around.

Next, we felt it was important we were very clear about when we would consider terminating a pregnancy. We understood it would be a lot more difficult to be objective if I was already pregnant, so talking about it now was imperative. Finally, we decided we were going to try for six months to get pregnant, and that would be it. Our stipulations were signed, sealed, and delivered.

Next, we moved on to logistics. Safi's commitment to the military was quickly coming to an end. Until then, we knew he might still get deployed but if he did, it would be a short trip. Even if he left while I was pregnant, he would still be back for the birth.

We also decided reenlisting once his commitment was over was not within the realm of possibility given Soraya's special needs. To be honest, I'd felt like this decision was a no-brainer even before she was born. Safi loved the camaraderie of the navy, but he also knew my goals in life did not include being a military wife and that I still wanted to take over my dad's practice if possible.

As far as that dream went, we knew we'd have to tweak that original plan to fit our situation now. I wanted to get a handle on what was doable and what wasn't. Back when I was training in Toledo, one of my former attending physicians had a child with a complex genetic condition, so I called to ask his advice about what families in our situation should consider when planning our future. Although his child had passed, he told me how happy he was to have had *all* his children. He'd since created a foundation in his son's name, which put his pain into purpose. I took his words to heart and filed his message away for future reference: pain can be repurposed, and even children who aren't in this world as long as we'd like them to be, are a blessing.

"I'm so sorry you're going through this," he told me at the end of our conversation. "If you decide to move to Toledo, I'll create a position for you. You were always a fantastic resident, you're an incredible pediatrician, and we'd love to have you here." It was a relief to know I had an excellent job prospect if Toledo became a top contender.

We were at the airport coming back from our trip from Miami when we got an email informing us that Soraya's muscle biopsy was negative. Although we were disappointed that we still did not have a diagnosis and path forward for her medical issues, what we did have was exciting: confirmation that we would be unlikely to pass whatever it was along to another child. We could move forward with trying to have another baby!

Mama Mary had warned me we weren't going to get an answer from the test. Per usual, she was right. She has always been lovingly honest in communicating what she sees to me, and this situation was no exception.

Soraya was now officially a medical mystery. As physician parents, we knew it was going to be incredibly difficult to create an effective treatment plan without an official diagnosis, we also knew we'd done every test possible and ruled out every life-shortening disease. We were at the end of the line.

It was time for our family to move on. To leave the question of *why* behind us. To enjoy what Soraya *could* do and not what was difficult or impossible for her.

It. Was. Time.

Personal insight: Safi and I were in tunnel vision when it came to finding a diagnosis. The light at the end of the tunnel was this muscle biopsy. We put everything into the appeal process: letters from Soraya's physicians, contacting Congress, asking our physicians to do peer-to-peer conversations, and it worked! Not only did we get it approved, we changed the coverage policy so any person under military insurance could be approved for a muscle biopsy.

However, after seeing Soraya's pain post biopsy, we paused. We had to take a step back and reassess how long and at what cost we would pursue further testing.

Universal take away: When you are so driven to get results in a medical diagnosis (or anything in life), pay attention to the emotional and physical toll it may be taking on those involved. Every goal deserves a pause and reassessment.

Chapter 18

Float On

With the negative result allowing us to move forward with confidence, Safi and I started trying for a baby. We now were very clear that we were not trying to replace Soraya no matter what her long-term prognosis turned out to be. We weren't trying to provide another "helper" for Yasmeen to care for her sister. We simply knew we had more than enough love to give another child, and I was yearning for another chance at experiencing a typical babyhood and toddlerhood.

Six months later we succeeded in conceiving just as we were coming to the end of our self-imposed time limit. Our genetic counselor was the very first person we told the happy news. I wanted to be monitored closely from the very beginning just in case any issues started showing up early, like they had when Soraya measured well below her gestational age throughout the entirety of my pregnancy.

The next people we told were our parents, who were unaware of our efforts to have another child or that it was even a thought in our minds. Our announcement was met with little excitement and was received with far less joy than Yasmeen's or Soraya's. The nonreaction made me profoundly sad. It was like something else was being taken from us yet again—this time, our happiness about having another child.

Safi's parents at least congratulated us. When I told my parents, my dad appropriately cried with happiness, but my mom went and sat on the stairs and pouted. "Why are you doing this?" she demanded to know. "You didn't mean to, right?"

"Yes, we meant to," I replied.

"You know better," Mom told me with finality.

"Mom, I'm married. This was very planned, and this baby is very wanted."

She shook her head sadly. "Your hands are already so full. You're barely getting by as it is right now, and you're constantly having me and your sister fly in. I don't know how you're going to do this, but I'm not going to be able to help you this time."

Her words cut like a knife right through my heart. I'd never realized my mom resented my requests for help before this, but her complaint was now fully registered and there was no taking it back. I made a conscious, deliberate shift in that moment to allow her to simply be Grandma and no longer a caregiver going forward. Looking back, I think my mom was likely mourning the carefree experience she expected to have as Soraya's grandparent. While she could have communicated that to me in a kinder and gentler way, I really have no judgments about this anymore. Chronic illness has a way of wearing everyone down and revealing the less than best versions of ourselves.

Although Safi and I thought we had covered every possible angle related to having another baby, we were fully unprepared for the judgment that came with our pregnancy. Even people outside our families felt free to tell us whatever they were thinking, with multiple people asking me if my pregnancy was "an accident." I can only assume we were being judged as parents because we already had a child with special needs.

In my practice, I now care for a handful of large families who have not just one but several children with special needs. Before getting pregnant, I definitely would have thought, *What are they doing? How can they handle this?* After this experience, though, I will never again judge a person with a complex child for choosing to have another one. I know what that feels like, and it's honestly devastating. The truth is that the dream is never going to look the way we expect it to.

All I knew was that for us, this child would bring in more love, and we were capable of more love. After that, whenever anyone would say something along the lines of "Wow, you're really going to have your hands full," my new script became "Yup, and we're going to have our hearts full, too."

We ended up going to a civilian ob/gyn, something I was adamant about. I wanted to be checked whenever I needed or wanted to be, not just the few times that the military deems necessary. I chose a nice, patient, caring, giant teddy bear of a man for the job. He was exactly what I needed, and I would have him deliver 10 more babies for me if I could.

Usually, pregnant women don't get to see their OB until they're six weeks along, but at four weeks and three days I demanded an appointment. Once I gave the doctor a history of Soraya's birth, he immediately said, "Come on in now, and then we'll have you come back again next week, and the week after. I'll also get maternal fetal medicine and a high-risk OB involved immediately."

Despite our fears, I had a normal, run-of-the-mill, everyday pregnancy. Everything happened when it was supposed to happen. All my tests came back fine. Ultrasounds looked normal. The size of the baby was within the appropriate range from day one. Of course, I still worried about something going wrong, but the whole nine months, everything seemed to be going right.

Well, at least until it came time to deliver. Then things got extremely scary, extremely fast. It was the day after Christmas. I'd had an epidural with both of my previous deliveries, but my body reacted differently to it this time. My heart rate dropped dangerously low, and the doctors had to keep giving me medication to bring it back up.

By the third time I bottomed out, I knew the situation was not going well. Both the anesthesiologist and my OB were in the room, and typically they wouldn't have made an entrance until it was time to push. I was given two options: either I could have the baby naturally or I could give the epidural one more try, knowing there was a strong chance my heart rate would plummet seriously again, and I could be rushed to the OR for a C-section.

"I don't want to lose you," Safi told me, his eyes wide with fear. "I need you to do this naturally."

"Fine," I replied, resigned to doing whatever was needed to get this baby out safely. "I'll do it." Having a natural childbirth was never my goal as it is for so.many women, serving as just another reminder that things rarely go the way we plan.

Safi took my hand and stared deeply into my eyes. "And I want you to promise me one more thing: we are *never* doing this again. I don't care how much we love this baby and if they're the easiest kid on earth. We are never getting pregnant again."

As I felt the pain of every movement, I repeated his words like a mantra in my head: *we are never getting pregnant again.* The whole delivery, I kept thinking, *I can do this; it's my last time.*

Soon, the beautiful, joyous moment I'd always wanted to experience during Soraya's birth but hadn't gotten occurred. Leena Zarina (Safi's brother Sami got to choose our child's middle name this time) came into this world happy and healthy and with a vigorous, immediate cry. I looked down at her and decided she was the most beautiful thing I'd ever seen.

I started breastfeeding Leena in the hospital and she latched on right away. I was elated I'd have the experience I dreamed of, while also "winning" the deal I'd made with Safi back in Miami! A few hours later, though, we learned she had borderline jaundice. I held my breath that it would resolve itself quickly, but 24 hours later it was still present, and I had to admit defeat. And beyond winning

130

Keep Your Head Up

or losing, I knew Safi was right. I needed to be present for all three children and monitor my mental health. Of course, I was sad about not being able to breastfeed Leena like I'd wanted to, but I'd given my word and now had to follow through.

Leena's birth brought a sense of relief and calm to our family that we hadn't felt in years, if ever. While most people get overwhelmed when there's a new baby in the house, for us it almost felt like there was less stress. Having more chaos in our lives enabled us to relax and let go of whatever false sense of control we had left by this point.

It also seemed to even the playing field for everyone. When Soraya was born, my attitude with Yasmeen—unfair as it had been—was *you're healthy, you've already made it, you're going to win at this thing called life, I have to focus on Soraya*. Now, knowing Leena was a newborn who needed caring for as well, Soraya could no longer be the sole recipient of my undivided attention. I was even able to stop fixating on everything she did: *is her eye doing something weird? Is that eyelid a little bit lower? Is her hand okay? Is she making abnormal movements? Is that a seizure?*

Adding to our sense of relief was the upcoming shift in our professional lives that would allow us to make a welcome move. My commitment to the National Health Service Corps was coming to an end, as was Safi's commitment to the military. While we'd done some initial chatting about where we might head next, it was now time to seriously map out where we wanted to settle down permanently as a family. Safi and I had already interviewed in Grand Rapids, which is an hour and a half from where I grew up, as well as in South Bend, which is even closer to my parents' house. We liked aspects of both places and could see ourselves being happy in either.

Suddenly, though, it dawned on us that we needed to make sure *all* the pediatric specialties Soraya required were readily available before we committed to either destination. Before now, I think we both assumed that anywhere we went would be as good if not better than Virginia. I dove deeply into researching our options, and while both places were sufficient for Soraya's current health status, we'd likely have to head to a big-name, big-city hospital for care if her condition worsened. All I could think was *how I am going to hold down a job in rural Michigan if Soraya needs medical services that are only available in Chicago or Indianapolis?*

I needed an unbiased opinion to help determine the best choice for our family. I knew if I asked my parents, they would advocate for us coming home and as much as I wanted to be close to them, I realized it would probably not be in Soraya's best interest. Given her complex medical history, it was imperative we chose an area that had wide-ranging, top-notch, cutting-edge therapies and subspecialties close by.

I reached out to my mentor from my first pediatric rotation in South Bend. After hearing our story, she said, "You have a child who is undiagnosed and while she's doing well, you have no idea what the future holds. She needs to be near an A-plus institution, and I would give the children's hospitals in both places you're looking at a B-minus." She felt it would be hard for us to consult all the subspecialties Soraya needed on a regular basis in either place and recommended we consider where the absolute best children's hospitals are located: Denver, Philadelphia, Chicago, Boston, or Cincinnati.

This conversation totally shifted the way Safi and I were thinking about our family's future. Sadly, we had to acknowledge that South Bend or Grand Rapids were out of the running and that we were going to have to adjust the way we were conducting our job search. Whereas we'd always pitched ourselves as a package deal before, we decided Safi was going to have to take the lead this time. I told Safi, "You find a job first, and I'll figure it out from there."

I was still planning on working, not only to contribute to our family's income and for my mental health but also because there was no way I'd come this far only to hang it up now. That would have been a whole other piece of grief I was not willing to voluntarily

132

Keep Your Head Up

take on. It was bad enough I wouldn't be able to take over my father's practice as I'd always dreamed. Giving up being a doctor entirely was just too much to handle.

The plan now was for me to look for a job that could accommodate a part-time work schedule. It had been next to impossible to hold down a full-time job and still get Soraya to all her appointments. I had done it out of necessity for the past two years, but it had been hellish and something needed to give. I was willing for that something to be me.

This decision was not based on following traditional gender roles but because Safi's job brought in more money—and despite having insurance, Soraya's therapies cost *a lot* of money. In thinking about our life together, we'd known our arrangement could never be 50-50 all the time, and especially now, the idea of things being equal was just not possible. We discussed the importance of not keeping tally marks and agreed this was what we both needed now.

Unfortunately, many of the cities my mentor had suggested were incredibly expensive and given that I was now going to be working part-time, our income was not going to cut it in those places. Safi and I then decided it would be best to focus our job search in Cincinnati. It was a known quantity to us since I'd done part of my residency and Safi had done his full fellowship there. It also had a friendly, small-town vibe and was the closest we were going to get to my parents while still being able to afford the cost of living.

Safi called his mentor and explained our situation. Although they weren't looking for a partner, they knew my husband was a brilliant surgeon, hard worker, and talented academic. His mentor pitched the hospital on the idea of adding another hand surgeon to the team. The practice really advocated for him, and it worked.

Knowing Safi had an excellent position secured, I went to work on finding a part-time job in the area. Pretty soon, I had it narrowed down to three options: working at an underserved clinic at Cincinnati

Children's, a more upscale clinic in the suburbs with lots of amenities, or the pediatric practice of my mentor from my first rotation back in South Bend. Each had its advantages and disadvantages, and I really struggled with the decision.

The clinic at Cincinnati Children's saw patients from underserved communities, which had always been my passion. It included teaching in the academic setting, which I was also very interested in pursuing. On the practical side, the insurance coverage was incredibly generous and would certainly pay for much more than our military insurance had. The drawback was the academic publishing requirement, which would have meant doing a lot of work outside my regular hours. While my soul yearned for an underserved patient population and to teach at the institution that had trained me, I didn't know if I'd be able to keep up with the demands of being in academic medicine given Soraya's needs.

The high-end clinic offered a great salary and insurance coverage and wouldn't require any hours beyond those scheduled. It had every amenity known to man including a lactation specialist, and the patients all had insurance and were generally well-off. It was a lovely office full of well-trained medical people. The downside? The job didn't match my soul's purpose anywhere near as closely as the first opportunity.

And then there was the job with my mentor. Like Safi's mentor, she didn't really need another pediatrician in her practice but said she would find a place for me anyhow. I liked her office. There was a good mix of patients in it. If I wanted to teach, I could take on a resident but would not be required to do work beyond the hours for which I was scheduled and paid. It was a no-frills, no-fluff kind of job that fit my needs, with the added benefit of working for someone I already knew and loved.

In the end, Mama Mary helped me choose the winner. She said if I took the job at the clinic at Children's, I would end up doing even *more* than what was expected. I would likely become so invested in the residents that I'd be hosting dinners at my house and inviting people over all the time. And the act of making myself constantly accessible to everyone would really affect my ability to be more present at home, which was one of my goals. I knew she was right, so as much as this one might have turned out to be my dream job, it was going to have to be a no.

Mama Mary also foresaw the potential for legal issues at the fancy clinic. Surprise, surprise, a few months after we moved to Cincinnati, a scandal rocked the practice. Then, it got bought out. Again, it was a good thing I listened to her advice and passed on that job.

With those two ruled out, working for my mentor's practice was the only appealing option left. Mama Mary gave it her blessing, deeming it the best fit given our situation. She felt it offered the most support on our journey with Soraya, so it was a done deal. I happily accepted the offer.

When I told my parents we were choosing Soraya, and therefore Cincinnati, over everything—even the plan we'd so carefully devised about me taking over my dad's practice one day—they were heartbroken. Of course, they understood why we'd made our decision, but that didn't mean it was any easier for them to accept. Embedded in our culture is a child's responsibility to care for their aging parents, and Safi and I had truly wanted to take on that role for them. We'd envisioned a whole life with my family, possibly even buying a piece of land and building them a house on it, and now that wouldn't be happening either.

It was just another death of a dream.

Personal insight: While I didn't have a healthy child, there were still dreams I hung onto that I thought would be unaffected. I grieved the child that I thought I would have, but did not realize how having Soraya changed the course of my life, including where we'd live, how we would work, and family planning. At the time,

135

Float On

letting go of all those dreams felt awful and I was mourning so much the life I imagined.

Universal takeaway: Sticking to an original plan at all costs does not get you a trophy! Essentially there's no winning at life for not changing your dreams. This can apply to birthing plans, breast-feeding, family planning, careers, and so on. Let's not judge ourselves (or others) when releasing prior ambitions and welcome the shifts that are necessary to evolve into the life we were destined for.

Chapter 19

The 7th Element

Because Safi's navy commitment was not over for several more weeks by the time we were scheduled to move to Cincinnati, our fabulous former nanny helped me lug all the kids there and get us settled into our new home. Yasmeen was now six, Soraya was three, and Leena was six months old. I was hopeful we were leaving a sad and stressful past in Virginia and entering a happier, healthier, easier phase of life in Ohio.

Using our vast network of professional colleagues and contacts, Safi and I had handpicked all the new doctors we wanted in charge of Soraya's care in Cincinnati. We polled everyone we knew—and everyone they knew, and everyone they knew—looking to find the smartest, most talented practitioners in every subspecialty. After a long and exhaustive search, we thought we'd handcrafted a total A-team that had come with glowing recommendations.

Because we wanted to get Soraya established with them as quickly as possible, I'd scheduled appointments six months in advance, so she'd be seen immediately on our arrival. Safi even drove into town after a long shift to join me at the genetics appointment because we had put so much hope into this one doctor. With her fresh eyes on Soraya's complicated medical history, we anticipated learning something new about the confounding constellation of symptoms and possibly how to treat them more effectively.

Instead, the doctor strode into the room and announced, "I reviewed Soraya's chart, and it looks like you guys are all set."

Safi and I looked at her with our mouths hanging open. Seeing our bewildered expressions, she continued, "Well, you already had quite the workup in Virginia. My conclusion is that science just hasn't caught up to Soraya yet, and sometimes that's just the way it is. It's up to you if you want her to see a geneticist from here on out, but I think you're good."

In my experience, the one thing a physician can always do is listen and care. Even when there is no diagnosis or solid answer to offer, it is our responsibility to be invested in at least *trying* to help. I don't know what else was going on in that doctor's life that made her think my kid was "all set," but I truly believe she could and should have done better. However, I also believe compassion cannot be taught. While this doctor may have been brilliant and considered the top in her field, her practice had no heart to it.

As I sobbed in Safi's shoulder after that failed appointment, I thought, *We moved our whole life for this? My husband drove through the night just for us to get dismissed? Why can't anyone understand how hard we're working to make our daughter's life better? Is this move going to turn out to be a "grass is always greener" situation?*

A similarly disappointing encounter happened with the first endocrinologist we took Soraya to see. I had barely gotten done explaining that we were hoping for some insight into a blood sugar issue we'd seen on two random occasions in Virginia when he shut us down even more quickly than the geneticist. In fact, he used her dismissal of us as evidence that he should blow us off, too. "I already talked to the geneticist you saw," he told us. "She sees nothing to add here, and therefore I have nothing more to add as well."

Later, this same doctor established a clinic called the Center of Excellence within Cincinnati Children's Hospital, which was designed to attract and help undiagnosed patients from all over the world. Our pediatrician believed Soraya was the perfect candidate for the program, so she applied in her name. Of course, we were all shocked when it got rejected. When the pediatrician asked why, the endocrinologist admitted he was only taking patients he could find a diagnosis for so his numbers looked better. Safi the spicy meatball gave that endocrinologist a piece of his mind, saying something along the lines of "I'm sorry we weren't straightforward and easy enough for you to figure out, but you're essentially doing a disservice to all these families, not just mine. It's ridiculous for you to stack the numbers. As a researcher, you should know better."

Despite these few bad eggs, though, many of our new doctors in Cincinnati proved to be excellent. Our biggest win was the feeding team. At the forefront of their field, they designed Soraya a recipe of real pureed food for the G tube instead of only PediaSure. This meant she had a more concentrated, solid diet throughout the day, allowing for a much more flexible feeding schedule, the free exploration of foods and drinks any time of day, and the elimination of nighttime feeds.

This one change made an immediate difference. As soon as Soraya started getting real nutrition, her nails got stronger, her hair got thicker, and best of all, her speech improved drastically. Of course, the downfall was that Soraya was now fully dependent on the G tube for her nutrition. This was an especially hard thing for me to swallow—pun intended—but I was truly okay with this choice because it meant a better quality of life for my child.

Just as we were moving full speed ahead with finding new doctors and therapies to help Soraya, she started surprising us with the things she could do. She started walking more confidently without the stander. This quickly morphed into her learning how to walk backwards and even jump. Our minds were blown, and we prayed things would continue this major upward trajectory without the kind of plateauing we'd seen before.

And then there was her speech. After being so delayed, this was now taking off as well. Of course, Soraya being able to hug me back had been wonderful, but hearing her say *Mommy, I love you* was probably the sweetest sound I'd ever heard. I thought, *I'm so lucky my complex kid can not only be affectionate but can also verbally communicate.*

By now, I'd come to terms with the fact that Soraya was never going to be a so-called typical kid. As a pediatrician, I knew based on what I see with premature babies that if a child has not "caught up" by age two, it was simply not going to happen. But whereas before I had often worried what Soraya's capabilities might be—*Is she going to be a vegetable? Will she ever walk? Is she going to be verbal?*—now, as her sparkly personality and a constant flow of words emerged, it was like we'd been granted more than we had ever dared hope for her.

In fact, it almost started to feel like we now needed to justify why we were continually pushing for answers about her condition. I understood that the clinicians in the country's top children's hospital were used to seeing kids who had it far worse than Soraya, but we'd moved here to find an answer. And as parents, we felt we deserved one. Unfortunately, it would not be coming anytime soon.

Or ever.

Personal insight: We had put such high expectations on our first couple of physicians when we moved. We felt so deflated after those appointments and it made us second-guess even trying to get more answers for Soraya. Luckily, those experiences were few compared to the many incredible doctors we had. These encounters really helped us with our presumptions going into future appointments.

Universal takeaway: When it comes to searching for the best physician, all the accolades in the world doesn't always mean they're the best fit for you. This is a *hard* realization for me as a physician, as I assume the best of my colleagues. I have learned this may come from a difference in personality, research/career motives, compassion fatigue, or physician burnout. Regardless, don't put too much weight and hope in any one physician based on their exceptional credentials!

Chapter 20

Mr. Brightside

Safi and I were on the same page about sending our kids to public schools, so our home was purchased based on the schools it fed into. The area where it was located boasted a top school system known for being great with neurotypical as well as special needs kids.

We supplemented Soraya's regular public preschool experience with a program affiliated with Cincinnati Children's. Essentially, it was a preschool for special needs kids that emphasized social interaction while also providing physical, occupational, and speech therapy in a classroom setting. Soraya needed all those modalities and really thrived in the presence of her peers. I loved the idea of consolidating our time and doing therapy in a social setting. It was a perfect fit all around.

To be accepted at this program, a child had to be far off the norm in terms of cognitive ability. In this respect, Soraya had gained skills that were well beyond many of the children there. Even in her "regular" preschool, which had a 50-50 split between neurotypical and special needs children, she rated highly. At our first public preschool parent-teacher conference, the teachers tried to soft-pedal Soraya's test scores to me, expecting me to be sad about them. They were surprised to learn that I was overjoyed. "You have to understand, I didn't think she could do any of this, but she is!" I crowed.

Because there were so many parts of Soraya's condition that others cannot easily see, Soraya often "passed" as a neurotypical kid. She didn't have any behavioral issues. Students didn't get meals at school, so no one knew about the G tube. She was walking and talking within a typical range for preschool kids. When our children were playing outside, neighbors usually had no idea Soraya was a special needs kid.

This concept of "passing" frustrated me to no end. It meant I had to constantly advocate for Soraya during individualized education program meetings and hospital visits and that no one could see how long and hard Soraya had had to work to get to this place. I was learning quickly what strong biases people have about what a disability should look like.

Recognizing all of Soraya's successes, our new geneticist started pushing us to think about what her future might hold. "Where do you see Soraya's life in a year? In five years? In 10 years?" he asked us.

Up until then, we'd never had the luxury of looking beyond today, tomorrow, and next month. We'd gotten so stuck in the daily grind of feedings, school, and therapies, we didn't stop to consider what Soraya's long-term life might look like. The doctor's question provided such an a-ha moment for us: it was time to let go of the thought of her dying and start focusing on how she was *living*.

Honestly, my first thought was *I envision a 12-year-old kid in a diaper*. Thankfully, Safi spoke up with a more hopeful picture. "Soraya is going to live with us forever," he replied firmly.

"But what if she wants to live independently or be in a group home?" the doctor continued, adding that some of his patients with Down syndrome that lived in group homes had even gotten married.

Despite the hopeful image, Safi was downright livid that anyone could imagine Soraya not wanting to live at home. We had never even considered someone else caring for her. In our culture, we don't even put elderly relatives in nursing homes, no less our children, so to him, there was no other answer. In fact, we already had a plan with our financial advisor about moving into a ranch house to better accommodate Soraya's needs as she grew, and now this doctor was talking about group homes? It was a totally new concept.

And the geneticist was not done stymying us yet. "Look, Soraya is doing great. As a family, it's time to determine how far you want to go in trying to figure out the cause of her symptoms. Do you want to take her out of therapy and pretend like nothing's happening? Do you want to keep doing all these appointments and therapies, but then not look any further? Or do you want to keep going until no stone has been left unturned—and at what cost?"

It was another good reflection point. We decided we still wanted to turn over every stone we could medically without hurting Soraya. We also promised we'd start to examine what her *own* life might look like—not the one we envisioned for her, with us, forever.

But by far the most shocking thing I learned from this conversation with the geneticist was the discovery that I had stopped dreaming since Soraya's birth. A lot of parenthood centers on the dreams we have for our children, and I hadn't dared to have any for her because I thought she was going to die. It was almost easier to not look past the next appointment or test result when death seemed the only logical conclusion. It's horrible to not have any expectations for your child, and I realized how much grief that had caused me.

After that, in our minds we stopped limiting what the future might hold for Soraya and began the process of creating another story for her. In this imagined someday, Soraya's health and abilities continued progressing in a positive way. Her social skills and cute personality landed her a job as a bagger at Kroger's Supermarket. She found love and married, maybe even while living in a group home, and had a long and happy life.

With every indication Soraya was going to survive past childhood, it was time for me to figure out how to acclimate in society and make new friends while caring for a complex child. It's hard to describe the sinking feeling I'd get when I had to give Soraya a G tube feeding in front of new people. Helping Yasmeen's playdates understand Soraya's condition, and special needs kids in general, was another minefield. Often, it felt easier to simply not invite anyone new into our inner circle than to have to repeatedly explain our unique situation. When a friend's son received a diagnosis of autism, we got very close, very quickly because finally, someone understood my situation: we were both in the same club of having a kid with special needs.

It was still a hard life, but we were settled into both our chaos and routine. Nothing was too unexpected or unknown. Our jobs were interesting and fulfilling. Yasmeen and Leena were doing well in school and daycare. Soraya continued to make gains through hard work and therapy, though her gains were inconsistent. Contrary to my fears, she got fully potty-trained while still in preschool. She even eventually learned to read, write, and work with numbers, things I never would have dreamed she'd accomplish.

And yet with all this positive trajectory in our lives, I had to admit that I was still desperately unhappy and depressed. I think my expectation had been that I was struggling because I didn't have enough time to do everything I needed to do. I thought once we understood Soraya wasn't dying, I'd suddenly be able to catch my breath. However, I realized now that even when Soraya wasn't acutely sick, everything still felt incredibly hard. I was still not feeling completely stress-free or ready to live life. I needed to figure out how to live and function with a child who was complex but not dying.

It was time to give therapy another try. I found the perfect match in Dr. Olivia, who not only showed up for our first appointment but every appointment after that. She was then and continues to be a blessing in my life, offering much-needed clarity and support throughout our entire journey.

In the past, I'd always viewed therapy as something people do only when they're struggling. Now even if I'm having a great day, I know I still need therapy. In fact, I believe everyone needs therapy unless they're a master at regulating their emotions and always have amazing coping skills. (And maybe there are people out there like that, but I don't know any!)

So now I was doing all the things: working, parenting, therapy, self-care. Because I'd struggled so much and worked so hard to get to this place, I started feeling like the world owed me something different than what I'd been given. I thought, *I've already paid my dues. I've gone through enough. I've worked through it all in therapy. From now on, my life is going to be perfect.*

After all, I was a well-respected pediatrician. I was married to a brilliant, talented hand surgeon. I had three beautiful daughters, all of whom I now expected to live long, happy, productive lives. I was living the dream.

What could go wrong?

Personal insight: Having the conversation with the geneticist was pivotal for Safi and me. It was the first time we were pushed to think about what Soraya's future might hold. It was the first time we stopped focusing on the daily grind to survive and were given permission to dream.

Universal takeaway: If you have a child with any type of disability, don't count them out! While you may continue to grieve the things that they can't do, allow them to surprise you. You don't need permission to re-create another dream.

Chapter 21

The World Has Turned and Left Me Here

In horror movies, there's a classic trope where everything seems fine for a short period of time—yet we all know the monster is still out there lurking about, just waiting for another chance to attack an innocent victim. This, as it turns out, was our reality. After lying in wait for several years, Soraya's medical monster crept back into our lives so slowly we wondered at first if we might be imagining it.

Our first clue was that Soraya's gait was somehow different. Now eight years old, she'd started hyperextending at the knee in a way she never had before, giving her an entirely new walking style. I took a video and sent it to her rehab doctor. He responded that it might be time for a more supportive type of brace.

But then she started to mention leg pain here and there. We noticed that she was getting more tired, more quickly than before. Her muscles seemed to become weaker and less able to hold her up. It became harder and harder to deny something was happening on a muscular level in her body.

Our team suggested we consult with a pediatric neuromuscular physician, so we made an appointment with the only one available in Cincinnati. I was comforted to realize I had met her briefly as a resident and knew her to be both talented and kind. This specialist felt the best course of action was to get an magnetic resonance imaging (MRI) of Soraya's legs, spinal cord, and brain. There are certain conditions this scan can pick up that other tests cannot, such as spina bifida. The doctor also wanted to do another muscle biopsy after the MRI results came in to see what was going on within Soraya's musculature.

The MRI was scheduled for the day after Thanksgiving, which was the only time both Safi and I could get off work. Yasmeen had come down with a terrible stomach bug two days prior and was still vomiting profusely when we left with Soraya for the test. Of course, I felt horrible leaving one sick child in the care of our nanny to attend to another, but Safi and I felt Soraya's extenuating needs necessitated us both being at the hospital with her.

The MRI went seemingly fine, but I noticed Soraya didn't look right in the car on the way home. I assumed she was still sleepy from the anesthesia, but even after we got inside, she never really came to. I took her temperature, and the thermometer read 106.8 °F. I took it again just to be certain. The same terrifyingly high number popped up.

Because of our medical training, Safi and I both were thinking that Soraya had malignant hyperthermia, a deadly response to anesthesia. In this reaction, patients spike a fever and then their body begins to stiffen. Without prompt hospitalization, the next step in the process is death.

"Do you want me to call 911?" I asked Safi.

"That will take too long," he replied. "Get in the car. We need to get her to the ER *now*." It usually takes 23 minutes to get to the hospital with no traffic, but Safi got us there in 13. We figured if the police pulled us over, they would help with the medical emergency rather than giving us a ticket.

In the emergency room, Soraya was taken directly to the trauma bay. I still have nightmares about caring for patients in the trauma bay as a resident: The near-fatal car accidents, accidental amputations, the drownings, the hangings. Back then, we had to take turns carrying the trauma pager and when it went off, we oversaw the entire show. We had to know what to say, what to do, what lines to get, and what labs to ask for as fast as possible and do it all decisively because someone's life was always at stake. It was a high-pressure, scary environment as a doctor, but even more so as a parent of a patient.

Soon, the chaplain was called into the room. I knew what that meant, and I cannot begin to describe the terror and sorrow I felt in that moment. Eventually—thankfully—doctors managed to stabilize Soraya. Although her heart rate and fever continued to soar, they at least no longer believed her death was imminent.

Soraya was admitted to the hospital and put on a plethora of monitors. Her blood sugar dipped dangerously low even though I had given her a G tube feeding on the car ride home. She was dehydrated. None of her symptoms made any sense or added up to any specific cause.

Doctors looked at her lungs for possible pneumonia. They took a multitude of blood cultures and examined her urine. No infection was found anywhere in her body. We now know this frightening and serious reaction was brought on by anesthesia, which Soraya's body reacts to by going into shock. Initially, this negative health spiral was only triggered when she was under for longer periods—it had been three long hours for that MRI—but these days, any anesthesia at all will do it.

Although the current crisis was over, Safi and I still didn't feel safe leaving Soraya in the hospital alone. Unfortunately, Yasmeen was still vomiting at home, the nanny needed to leave, and my aunt was flying in from Bangladesh to meet Soraya and Leena for the first time. We called one of our lovely and qualified backup babysitters to ask her to please manage things for us back at home. She totally came through, giving up a Friendsgiving and other fun holiday plans for us. As always, the kindness of others toward our family continued to astonish and humble me.

149

The World Has Turned and Left Me Here

I rushed home to get extra clothes and toiletries, bringing back all of Soraya's medical records with me when I returned. I stayed up all night looking for clues about these latest symptoms. Why was her gait changing? Why were her legs hurting? Why was her blood sugar so erratic? I found no answers, as always.

The next day, Safi brought Leena and Yasmeen to visit Soraya at the hospital. Honestly, and maybe selfishly, I just wanted to make sure Yasmeen was okay because she had been sick. I never stopped to consider the impact the visit might have on her.

Soraya was still connected to a bunch of monitors, but she was on the upswing. Leena, who was just turning four, took it all in stride. Yasmeen, who was nine and understood so much more than her little sister, was more affected. After Soraya was discharged, Yasmeen told me fiercely, "I never want to go back to that hospital again." It wasn't the first time she'd made that kind of statement, and I knew we'd have to honor her request going forward.

Many people believe siblings of special needs kids are amazingly empathetic, and that's true. But what they may not realize is they also harbor some strong and very understandable resentment toward their siblings. This current situation added a whole new layer to Yasmeen's already conflicted feelings about Soraya.

Yasmeen missed her home, friends, and school in Virginia and was bitter we'd had to move for Soraya's health care needs. She wanted a normal life where she could have a friend over without having to explain anything. Soraya's sensory issues meant we could not go anywhere as a family that included crowds, loud noises, or large groups. As a result, Yasmeen never got to go to the amusement parks, restaurants, arcades, or school carnivals she would have loved to experience, leading to even more resentment toward her sister.

Like any sibling, Yasmeen loved her sister and sometimes hated her. But "hating" a sibling with special needs feels very wrong, which sent her into a torrent of self-loathing. All this chaos, fear, anger, and resentment soon spiraled into extreme anxiety and insomnia.

On top of all that, now there was not only the fear associated with having seen Soraya so ill but also enormous feelings of abandonment. I'm sure Yasmeen was thinking, *When I get sick you leave me here vomiting, but when Soraya gets sick you rush out the door with her.* We regularly took time off work for Soraya's therapies, appointments, surgeries, and biopsies but never to do something fun with her. She must have felt shoved aside.

I'm also sure she'd picked up on our stress. She'd seen us cry on a regular basis. This was not likely what most other kids her age were experiencing at home.

I'm going to be honest—I was not too pleased when Yasmeen's therapist, whom she'd been seeing since we'd moved to Cincinnati, suggested she might benefit from taking an antidepressant. I asked our pediatrician for a second opinion, and she agreed with the therapist.

I was still fearful but also realized Yasmeen needed help coping with her big feelings. Neither apologizing for our parenting choices nor all the therapy, love, and support in the world was going to erase the images and thoughts she was trying to process in her mind. More than anything, I just wanted her to be able to sleep, go to school, and live without resenting her sister, and, more important, hating herself so much. While I didn't know what the medication was going to do to her brain or what its lasting effects would be, I wanted to give her the chance to live with more joy and less misery.

We started our oldest on Zoloft at age nine. She may have been the first in the family with a prescription for an SSRI (selective serotonin reuptake inhibitor, aka an antidepressant), but she wasn't the last.

Personal insight: While I had the best intentions for Yasmeen to come visit Soraya in the hospital during Thanksgiving, I had never imagined the negative impact it would have on her. I had never thought about a sibling experience being so different from what I was experiencing. I had hoped therapy would be enough to help her. I was so resistant to Yasmeen being on medication due to my negative experience with it in medical school. My resistance resided in another disheartening realization: even my "healthy" child was not exempt from struggle.

Universal takeaway: Put extra focus on the mental health of siblings of those with any medical conditions. It is a population I never learned about in medical school. Acknowledge that their experience may be uniquely challenging. Start therapy proactively and be open to medication if your medical professional recommends it.

Chapter 22

Sleepyhead

Once we noticed Soraya's gait change, I was rightfully concerned about it but not thinking our whole life trajectory was about to change. After seeing her in the trauma bay and how quickly she'd declined after having anesthesia, though, I was less confident about life continuing along the way it had been. I didn't feel safe.

There was still a muscle biopsy to do, and it terrified me knowing Soraya was going to have to be under anesthesia again. But thinking the result might provide desperately needed answers regarding her latest health challenges, we forged ahead.

Still, we weren't taking any chances this time around. Prior to the procedure, we met with the head of anesthesiology at the hospital, who suggested treating Soraya as if she had mitochondrial disease during the procedure. Because people with mitochondrial disease process anesthetics differently, we thought this was a brilliant idea and quickly agreed. We also consulted an endocrinologist, who decided to equip Soraya with a blood glucose monitor after she left the hospital. That way, we'd have a method for tracking her glucose numbers and determining how long it took her body to recover from the anesthesia.

With these safeguards in place, we went ahead with the procedure and Soraya came through it like a champ. The blood glucose monitor taught us that it took her body two full weeks to get over the effects of anesthesia. We remained hopeful the test results would help us learn how to better treat and maybe even cure this mysterious new crop of symptoms.

The muscle biopsy came back, revealing several abnormal cells. However, none of the doctors could discern what those cells were or what they meant in terms of Soraya's health. It seemed everyone knew something wasn't right, yet no one knew exactly what was wrong. Now it felt like we were back at square one.

We decided to call a care conference with Soraya's entire medical team to brainstorm methods and medications that might help her going forward. This meeting was conducted over video, which became the norm less than a year later when the pandemic hit but still seemed innovative and unique at the time. On the call, it was recommended that we add to the team a rheumatologist and an oncologist with a specialty in HLH (hemophagocytic lymphohistiocytosis), a disease of a specific type of cells called *macrophages*. Some of these cells had been found in Soraya's biopsy, so both suggestions made sense to us. Other ideas tossed around by the doctors included doing steroid trials and using anti-cancer and anti-inflammatory medications to help ease Soraya's symptoms. We were on board with all these possibilities and felt each had the potential to help our daughter.

Toward the end of the meeting, the neuromuscular doctor who'd ordered the biopsy told us we might want to consult with the Mayo Clinic going forward because there was nothing more the neuromuscular department could offer us. The rest of the team seemed as appalled as we were by this declaration, and I later got an apology from Cincinnati Children's for this physician's behavior. I told the hospital representative, "I get it. That doctor has too many patients as it is. They can't figure Soraya out, so they're over it." It didn't make me any happier about a doctor's decision to simply give up on my child, but I certainly understood why it had happened.

By this point, we were regularly giving Soraya Tylenol for pain and continuously monitoring her blood glucose. We tried the prescribed steroid burst to help ease her growing list of symptoms, but even though they initially seemed to give her more energy, in the end they only made her more tired. During this intervention, she'd be able to climb stairs with no problem at the beginning of each day, but by nighttime she had to resort to crawling up them. The slow decline continued.

And then COVID hit. Instead of going to the hospital to do therapies, they were now being conducted virtually. As a result, it took longer than it usually would have for Soraya's physical therapists to notice she now had to lean against a wall for support between repetitions of her exercises or wasn't holding her head up as well as she had been.

Or that the length of time she was able to sustain her energy during therapeutic activities was getting shorter and shorter.

Or that because she was tired, she often needed to take a minute break between whatever skills they were trying to work on with her.

Everything just seemed like too much work for her now.

And as devastating as the pandemic was for everyone else in the world, its effects were multiplied exponentially for us as physician parents of a medically complex child. While the message to everyone else on the planet was *stay home*, the message to us health care workers was *Go be a hero!* I was like, *I don't want to be a hero! I want to stay home, too, and protect Soraya!*

Financially, though, this was simply not an option. Our livelihood depended on caring for patients out there in the big, scary universe, and now it seemed we might bring home a virus at any moment that could easily cost Soraya her life. I started getting that awful, sinking feeling and impending sense of doom again. To me, it honestly felt like the world was coming to an end.

155

Sleepyhead

I spiraled into a mire of incessant overthinking and nonstop worrying. I was so terrified of everything, I could barely get out of bed some days. I started having all the same feelings as when my dad was in the hospital: first my stomach would drop, then I'd go into a full-blown panic attack. I realized my body was trying to process the trauma of the past several years. While I wasn't in the same kind of deep, dark place I'd experienced when I was in medical school, I worried things would only get worse.

Soon, I was feeling so much stress and anxiety, I booked an appointment with my primary care doctor. After carefully listening to my situation, she suggested I try some medication. Initially, I balked at the idea. It's not that I'm anti-medication; it's just that I was terrified I might have the same experience as I did the first time I tried it in med school. Back then, I'd gone into the situation blindly, encountered every side effect there was, and had terrible withdrawal symptoms. I didn't want any of that to happen again.

My doctor gently pushed me to reconsider. "Go be an example for your kids." I realized my fear of medication was perpetuating a stigma and adding to a narrative I didn't want any part of and truly didn't believe in. I agreed, and I became family member number two with a prescription for an selective serotonin reuptake Inhibitor (SSRI).

Meanwhile, Safi was also starting to panic. Not only was he dealing with the same fears about being a health care worker during a pandemic but he was also going through a job change that necessitated his entire department transition to a new hospital system. The associated financial insecurity, job uncertainty, risks to Soraya's health, and watching her active decline became too much for him. Seeing my very grounded, always logical rock of a husband fall apart made the world seem even scarier to me. I asked him to be vulnerable enough to admit that he was not the best he could be and needed help.

Safi's previous lens regarding therapy had been *it's fine for you because you've had that label of depression, and you are at higher risk. It's fine for Yasmeen because she is a child trying to manage her emotions through a very serious, very saddening adult situation. But I don't need therapy because I don't have any of that baggage.* In his mind, he was never "bad enough" to require help. I think what finally got him to agree to therapy and later medication (family member number three on an SSRI!) was when I told him, "If you think therapy and medication are only reserved for hard situations, I can't think of one harder than what we're going through right now."

Of course, our worst fear was Soraya dying. We kept asking each other, "What if this is terminal?" Then the other one of us would quickly go into reassurance mode. "No, that's not what this is. We must be overreacting."

Truly, the only thing we knew for sure was that Soraya's symptoms were slowly but surely getting worse. We didn't allow anyone but our immediate family and Soraya's direct caregivers into our house because the risk of getting sick was just too high, so it was easy to hide what was happening behind closed doors. No one knew Soraya wasn't walking as much. No one knew how tired she was. No one knew she wasn't breathing as well. No one knew we were going through major changes as a family.

It was all just a giant secret we kept to ourselves.

Given Soraya's ever-increasing issues with fatigue and a new shortness of breath, I asked her pediatrician to add on a pulmonologist to her list of subspecialists. He saw us and ordered sleep study. The one she'd had several years earlier revealed mild sleep apnea that was treated with Flonase and other allergy medications. I thought perhaps she was more tired these days because the sleep apnea had progressed. If that was the case, it would be a quick fix: get her tonsils and adenoids out and presto! She'd be back to her spunky, sassy self in no time.

157

Sleepyhead

In addition to ordering the sleep study, our doctors suggested conducting a computed tomography (CT) scan of Soraya's lungs to ensure her lung processes were normal. Much like the time I took Soraya to the gastroenterologist without Safi because I assumed it would reveal nothing major, I decided this was a benign enough test that I could handle the appointment alone. No big deal, right?

I stood watching as Soraya entered the tube of the CT machine. She was lying there calmly, and I started to relax. Then the technician told her to take a big breath. This allows doctors to get a good view of the lungs during both inspiration and expiration.

Anything I expected to see happen in that moment was noticeably absent. There was little to no movement in Soraya's chest. Her ribs were not expanding. There was just ... nothing. In my mind, I consoled myself with the thought that I probably hadn't seen Soraya's chest moving simply because she had her shirt on.

At the end of the scan, I was told the result was normal. Soraya's lungs looked fine. Still, I couldn't get the picture of her chest wall muscles failing to move out of my mind. I was almost afraid to tell Safi about it because I thought it was just my overthinking anxious mind.

When I finally gave him a heads-up later in the day, he assured me he saw Soraya's muscles moving when she breathed. I remained unconvinced. I still saw only stillness where there should have been movement.

"Seriously, she's fine," he told me again.

"Let's play a game to be 100% sure," I suggested. "Let's say we need to check Soraya's G tube. I'll pull her shirt up and then we'll take a video of her breathing."

We had often asked Leena to come play doctor and patient with Soraya to make it more fun while we were doing real medical things, so this was par for the course. The girls suspected nothing, which was a good thing, because by this point, I was absolutely terrified.

After we were done "checking Soraya's G tube," Safi and I went to examine the resulting video while the girls continued to play happily.

We quickly noticed that when Soraya breathed, the only thing moving—if anything at all—was her belly. That meant she needed to engage muscles from places other than her chest to breathe correctly. I emailed the video to our doctor with a note saying, *I'm not sure if I should be concerned, but I'm not seeing Soraya's chest wall expand when she breathes. You're the pulmonologist, though, and I'd appreciate hearing your opinion.*

He responded immediately. It was 10:30 on a Sunday night. His attentiveness could only mean he thought this was a bigger problem than I'd even imagined.

We need to move that sleep study up, his message read. There was no mistaking the urgency in his words. The usual eight-month wait for a sleep study was reduced to less than a week.

It was reckoning time.

Personal insight: Our observations of Soraya's increasing fatigue, her changing gait, and ultimately her change in breathing pattern led to prompt evaluation. These observations paid off. It did seem like history was repeating itself with sending a video to the pulmonologist (similar to sending a video to the pediatrician of Soraya having feeding difficulties when she was a baby) and my lesson from that was to keep observing, as it would change the course of Soraya's care!

Universal takeaway: Parents know their children best. It's worth it to keep a list of observations to share with your medical team. You never know what may lead to a diagnosis or reason for what you are seeing. Trust your gut if something feels off even if it's not clear-cut and it's hard to explain.

Chapter 23

Just Breathe

Safi spent the night in the hospital with Soraya during her sleep study. While she dozed, he diligently recorded the numbers on the end-tidal CO_2 monitor (a machine that measures breath-by-breath carbon dioxide levels). Even before he shared the results with a dear friend who is a critical care doctor, he knew what they meant: Soraya's chest muscles were no longer effectively moving air through her lungs.

He texted me a crying emoji. As a surgeon who fixes things for a living, it was an incredibly hard pill to swallow. He was always saying he'd be fine if Soraya had the ability to breathe on her own, and now that bar had snapped.

When Safi and Soraya returned home the next morning, he looked like a broken man. Tough emotions were written all over his face: anger, sadness, frustration. Still unaware of how her life was about to change, Soraya was all smiles, relieved to be out of the hospital and back with her sisters.

As we waited for the pulmonologist to confirm what we'd already surmised, Soraya's school communicated that they'd been noticing some personality changes in her. The words used to describe her recent conduct were shocking: rude, disrespectful, irritable. We'd occasionally seen flashes of this at home and attributed it to growing fatigue and pain, but we never imagined it would start spilling over at school. As a pediatrician and mom, I know kids are far more likely to fall apart in the safe space of their family rather than in front of their peers and teachers. Our hopes fell yet another rung.

I did a quick search on the symptoms of hypoventilation (high levels of carbon dioxide in the bloodstream, which we now knew Soraya was experiencing). Fatigue, irritability, impulsivity, confusion, and forgetfulness were on the list. Check, check, check, check, and check. I emailed our pulmonologist to get his take on what was going on. His response was unequivocal: between the sleep study and worrisome behavior, a ventilator was a necessary next step in Soraya's care.

Safi and I fell into complete and utter defeat. Over the years, we'd thrown everything we had into finding the most effective treatments and technologically advanced testing for our little girl. She'd gone through a plethora of painful surgeries and spent countless hours learning how to do things most people take completely for granted—like eating, walking, and talking. And for what? Just to end up here, with no diagnosis, no effective treatment options, and at risk of losing all those hard-earned skills.

I pushed Soraya's care team to be frank about the situation going forward. "Clearly, I know there will be another step of decline."

"You don't know that," the doctors tried to reassure us. "Soraya could stabilize in this same place for the next 10 years."

"Tell me about someone who has been on the same vent settings for a decade, then," I pleaded, wanting to believe in their hopeful assessment. "What would that look like?"

The doctors told us about a muscular dystrophy patient who had been on a ventilator at night for many years. Very slowly over time, she'd started needing it for short windows during the day. Even more slowly, those windows had increased in length. They didn't say what happened next.

"Well, what if Soraya eventually needs it *all* the time?" I persisted.

"Then we'll talk about a tracheostomy" was the answer. The thought of Soraya having a tube inserted through her neck and into her windpipe was devastating. As a doctor, I know a trach changes everything about a patient's life—from how they eat, drink, and communicate to the activities they can participate in. I didn't want her to have to endure another complicated operation or additional piece of machinery. She'd already endured enough.

My stomach sank. I felt like this was the beginning of the end.

Both the pulmonologist and the pediatrician continued to emphasize the possibility that Soraya might maintain the current ventilator settings indefinitely. My experience—not to mention my gut—was telling me their rosy long-term scenario was highly unlikely. Soraya had recently asked me if she could take a nap while she was on the toilet, heralding in an entirely new level of exhaustion for her. Imagining her maintaining any level of strength seemed impossible.

"That doesn't seem probable given the new chest wall involvement," I countered. "Don't you agree this is different?"

When pushed, the doctors were forced to admit there was also a strong potential Soraya's muscles would continue to weaken, and they recommended consulting a neuromuscular specialist to gain further insight. Unfortunately, the only one at Cincinnati Children's had already released us from her care because she had "nothing more to add." There was zero chance we were going back to someone who had no interest in trying to figure out Soraya's case—and if we consulted someone else, it would only be the best of the best.

"I refuse to see a doctor who isn't committed to helping our child," I stated flatly.

"And we don't want 10 second opinions; we want one," Safi added, spicy as ever.

We were referred to the preeminent pediatric neuromuscular researchers at the National Institutes of Health (NIH) in Bethesda, Maryland. We knew we needed a miracle and hoped they could provide one for us. Due to the pandemic, though, the earliest appointment we could get was five months away.

Until then, our biggest concern was telling the girls and calming any fears they had about this latest development. When we broached the new machinery with Soraya, the first thing she wanted to know was "Will it make me better?"

We assured her it would make her less tired. Safi uses a continuous positive airway pressure machine at night, so we used that as a comparison. "Dad has his sleep machine, and this is your sleep machine," we told her. "Your doctors say it will help you have more energy during the day."

Soraya understood that her muscles were weak. She also knew people often work out to strengthen their muscles, and she hoped her ventilator would produce the same kind of results. "If I do this, will I get stronger?"

We were completely honest with her. "It will help while you're using it, but it won't permanently fix your muscles or make them grow."

Soraya didn't love the answer but accepted it. Her next biggest concern was sleeping with something on her face. She has sensory issues, so a mask covering her mouth and nose at night was a big deal. The pulmonologist let us take home different options to figure out which was the most comfortable, and we practiced putting the masks on and keeping them on for progressively longer amounts of time. It was a challenge, but she rose beautifully to the occasion.

We had separate conversations with Leena, who was 6 at the time, and Yasmeen, who was almost 12, to explain why their sister now needed an apparatus to breathe. As a visual aid, we drew a picture showing the mechanics of inhalation and exhalation: oxygen coming in, carbon dioxide (CO_2) going out. We shared that Soraya's weakened muscles were no longer able to push the CO_2 out of her

Keep Your Head Up

lungs fully, and we demonstrated how the new machine would assist in the oxygen exchange.

Hearing the news, Leena was ecstatic. She was grateful there was equipment to help her sister. She thought the doctors were fantastic to have recommended it.

Yasmeen felt very differently, not to mention strongly. "What's the cause of the muscle weakness?" she demanded to know.

When I said we had no idea, she thought we were lying. Back and forth we volleyed.

"You're not telling me something."

"No, we really don't know."

"You don't want me to know the truth."

"I swear we don't know anything more than what we're telling you."

Once we finally convinced her we weren't holding back any information, Yasmeen was livid. "Why isn't anybody working on this?!"

I told her we had an appointment scheduled with the NIH and would be seeing the top pediatric neuromuscular physicians in the world there. But I also had to break it to her that despite the top minds working on Soraya's medical mystery, it was still likely we wouldn't be getting any further answers.

"Soraya didn't need this machine last year, so why does she need it now?" Yasmeen persisted. "What happens if her muscles get even weaker?"

In that case, I told her Soraya would have to use the machine more often.

"So, she's eventually going to have to take it to school with her?" Yasmeen yelled, pushing even further into the imagined future. "It's not going to fit in her locker!"

I assured her that if Soraya ever needed the vent during the day, we'd send her to school with a portable one.

165

Just Breathe

"Well, what if she needs it 24 hours a day?" Yasmeen pressed on.

I explained that because wearing a mask continuously causes skin breakdown and other health concerns, continuous use isn't possible.

"What happens next, then?" she wanted to know.

"We'll cross that bridge when we come to it," I told her.

The nebulous answer wasn't going to cut it for my analytical eldest. She still wanted more explanation, so I asked her permission to tell the unvarnished truth. "Once you know this stuff, you can't unknow it," I warned. "Are you sure you want to hear it?"

Yasmeen assured me she did, and I believed her. Drawing another picture, I explained what a tracheostomy is. She was beside herself.

"What would Soraya's voice sound like if she got that?" she cried.

"We're not there yet," I said, trying to reassure her. My words provided little comfort, to her or to me. Yasmeen absolutely understood the progression of events now, whereas Leena and Soraya still did not. It was a heavy burden for her to bear.

When Safi found out the extent of our conversation, he was upset. "Why did you tell her that much?!"

"You trusted me as a pediatrician to speak to her," I told him. "With kids, you have to be very direct and matter of fact. She asked, and we went there."

I didn't regret being honest with Yasmeen, but I do regret the position it put her in. I'm sure it is no fun being half a child, half an adult, and she'd occupied that liminal space since Soraya was born. Again, this latest example wasn't what I would have chosen for her, but it certainly was nothing new.

We carried on.

Personal insight: With Soraya needing a ventilator, Safi and I learned to never hang on to "at least" statements. There have been so many times we had convinced ourselves that things could be worse (e.g. *at least she doesn't have a ventilator*). We clung to these beliefs to stay afloat and stay sane. Safi had always thought that he would be fine, just as long as her condition didn't affect breathing. I am not sure why we bargain with things that are out of our control, but I don't recommend it!

Universal takeaway: When comforting others in a tough situation, avoid saying anything that starts with *"Well, at least ..."* Examples of these include *"Well at least ... your child can breathe on their own, you're not divorced, your other children are healthy, you can have more children, and so on."* You get the point. You have no idea what is temporary and how much people may hang onto these beliefs to function.

Chapter 24

False Confidence

The ventilator helped with Soraya's fatigue almost immediately, but her irritability continued. She began picking at her skin to the point where she needed multiple bandages to cover the self-inflicted wounds. She had frequent outbursts that felt a lot like toddler tantrums. I was constantly asking myself, *Is this fatigue? High carbon dioxide levels? Pain?* It was hard to tell where one problem ended and another started.

At the time, our strategy was to wait for Soraya to tell us she was hurting before giving her medication. Managing this process was particularly challenging because she didn't always express herself in a timely manner. Often, by the time she complained, her pain was severe.

One night I said to Safi, "I really think we need to get palliative care involved."

He looked at me, horrified. "No! Absolutely not."

His lens is one of adult medicine—and in adult medicine, palliative care goes hand in hand with hospice. Because only patients with a six-month or less life expectancy are referred there, in Safi's mind, I'd just declared Soraya's condition terminal. He was having none of it.

I carefully explained to him that in pediatrics, palliative care does not necessarily equate to death. It simply acknowledges that chronic medical issues are not likely to improve and is designed to help manage symptoms, make patients more comfortable, and enhance their quality of life. These were things we both wanted for Soraya.

My initial thought was we would use their services purely for pain control. Palliative care doctors come from a different perspective and are very knowledgeable about using different combinations of medications. Most pediatricians have not been trained on pain management outside of Tylenol and ibuprofen—I know I wasn't—and ours was no exception.

Safi dug in his heels. "No palliative care. We don't need that."

Since our care team hadn't brought the idea up to us, I worried he was right. Maybe I was being overdramatic. I'd certainly been known to go down the worst-case scenario path on occasion, and I was willing to consider this was one of those times.

The next day, I called our pediatrician and pulmonologist to get their thoughts on the matter. I didn't mention the difference of opinion; I simply asked the question: "Is this an appropriate use of palliative care or am I being premature?"

They assured me it was a very fair use of the services. "But remember," I was reminded, "Soraya could be on these ventilator settings for the next 10 years."

"Let me explain what I'm really worried about," I continued, opening the door to our internal struggles. "At a certain point, I assume Soraya's muscle weakness may get to a point where we need to consider a tracheostomy—and the problem is, I can't even say that word in front of my husband without him falling apart. And if I can't say it, then we can't talk about it, so we're going to need some assistance."

Both doctors told me palliative care would be instrumental in facilitating the difficult medical and ethical conversations that came along with the surgery. Our general pediatrician agreed and thought having them oversee Soraya's pain would also be helpful since it was becoming increasingly difficult to keep it in check. We got the referral, and that was that.

I left those conversations feeling a mixture of empowerment infused with terror and guilt. I worried that I'd manifested something terrible and spiraled into a painful bout of overthinking. *How do you know for sure if you need palliative care? Maybe we're not there yet! Would someone else have brought it up to us if I hadn't said something first? Were they waiting for us to bring it up? How does this work?*

By the time I got the phone call to schedule the appointment, my heart was ricocheting around in my chest. I knew I'd asked for this, but the reality of it was terrifying. It would have been so much nicer if Soraya's care team had said, "You don't need that," but no one had.

Despite my tortured thoughts, Safi, Soraya, and I went to the appointment as scheduled. Safi was still reluctant to be there and most likely mad at me for pushing the whole thing forward. I was busy showing my false confidence because on the one hand, I was trying to justify that we needed this, and on the other, I was afraid we needed it. Soraya had no idea about the tension between us or the implications of being there, so she viewed it as another doctor's appointment in a long line of many.

We met with the team that had been assigned to us: Dr. Meyer, our palliative care physician, a fellow (a doctor training to become a palliative care physician), and a social worker. This team aspect highlights how palliative care takes a different approach from other specialties. When the three of them walked into the room together, it was so foreign that it felt intimidating and I wondered if we really needed to be there.

All that dissipated once we started talking. It felt like we were having a nice conversation—and possibly even therapy—as opposed to a doctor's appointment. "Tell us why you're here," Dr. Meyer began. "What can we help you with? What are your hopes for Soraya?"

I thought the best approach would be total transparency on my part. "What brought us here is Soraya's pain, but I'm a little nervous this is not appropriate. I don't know if I'm in the right place or if this is the right time. Is this really a club we're in now?" Between my awkward jokes, I got the point across in a way that Soraya thankfully did not pick up on.

Dr. Meyer and crew assured us that we were in the right place and club. That we'd come at the right time. And they could absolutely help us manage Soraya's pain more effectively.

"There's something else I wanted to ask ...," I continued. "If things progress the way I assume they will, we are going to need help navigating everything that goes along with that."

I did not utter the word *tracheostomy*. Soraya didn't know this was a possibility yet and Safi would no doubt turn on the waterworks. Once again, we were reassured that palliative care would be there to help us deal with difficult conversations and decisions regarding Soraya's shifting medical needs.

There was so much kindness emanating back at me, I gathered up the courage to ask yet another big question I'd been pondering but hadn't even brought up to Safi yet. I figured he was already mad at me for being here, so I had nothing to lose. "While we're talking about these kinds of things, I'd also love to know if we're a family that might qualify for Make-A-Wish."

Stunningly, the answer was again yes—and the sooner the better. The recommendation is always to fulfill a child's wish while they are still able to enjoy it as much as possible, given their diagnosis and symptoms. Since doctors had no idea how fast Soraya's muscle weakness would progress from here on out, the time was now.

We wrapped up with a plan to reconvene in six months, and in the meantime Dr. Meyer would collaborate with pulmonology

172

Keep Your Head Up

to manage Soraya's pain. We all left that meeting feeling like we'd found ourselves a new friend—even Safi. His resistance and anger had faded during the appointment, and he now saw how Dr. Meyer could be a great ally for Soraya.

Our family was slowly coming to an acceptance of Soraya's new medical needs—make that, everyone except Yasmeen. Her constant refrain was *This is so unfair. My friends don't have to go through this. Our neighbors don't have to go through this. So why does our family have to go through this?*

We'd already had multiple talks with her about how, as the saying goes, everyone is fighting a battle we know nothing about. We also acknowledged the truth of the situation. It was not fun or fair, and there was no need to pretend it was. Everyone was allowed to have strong feelings about it, and the expression of those feelings was encouraged.

At one point, Safi told her point-blank, "All of this sucks, and there's nothing else to do but embrace the suck."

His statement felt very honest and true. Yasmeen was temporarily appeased with the "embrace the suck" philosophy. The next day, though, her complaints of unfairness resurfaced.

Safi gave her an exasperated look. "What did I tell you yesterday?"

With a big sigh, Yasmeen replied, "Embrace the suck."

Seeing this phrase wasn't quite doing it for our eldest daughter, I chimed in. "I feel like we need a family motto, and I don't think it's *embrace the suck.*"

Safi thought for a moment, then snapped his finger. "Maybe it's *suck the joy out of life.*"

"Yes, that's it!" I agreed. "We have to be intentional about finding our joy. We can't wait for it to happen or for a time when we can finally 'be happy.' We have to go and get it now."

And just like the white light comforting baby Soraya had given us the strength to keep moving forward, the establishment of our family motto helped us march ever onward with a new attitude. We refused to waste any more time bemoaning our fate. We had to make every second count, because we didn't know how many more of them Soraya had left.

Personal insight: It seemed that everything we feared for Soraya was coming true. Her health was getting worse as evidenced by the addition of the ventilator, increased pain, and palliative care. As much as Safi was resistant to palliative care and I was fearful of manifesting an unpleasant reality, it was the best next decision. As a couple we identified a major roadblock in communication: we could not talk about a tracheostomy. We knew it was a logical progression in conversation, but we still couldn't muster up the courage to talk about it.

Based on the drastically different responses Yasmeen and Leena had to the addition of the ventilator helped me learn the breadth of services palliative care can provide.

Universal takeaway: There needs to be a better understanding of what palliative care does across all medical education and in patient care. What we don't know can significantly affect the course of care for our loved ones. Again, if you are in a situation where you don't know if they can be helpful, *don't be afraid to ask.*

Chapter 25

Good Life

We held a family meeting to introduce Leena and Soraya to our new slogan. From moment one, the girls were fully on board. The only problem was, we didn't quite know how to put it into practice yet. Fear was still blocking our path.

It didn't help that the National Institutes of Health (NIH) had nothing new to say about Soraya's medical issues. While the neuromuscular team had been beyond wonderful, their evaluation—comprehensive testing that included magnetic resonance imaging, electromyography of the muscles, pulmonary function testing, blood work, and an echocardiogram—didn't yield anything new. Like all the other gifted medical professionals we'd consulted before, they were stumped by her dizzying constellation of symptoms and unable to recommend any treatment options to stave off further decline. While we were glad we'd made the trip and hoped our efforts might be able to help someone else in the future, we found ourselves right back in the same place where we started.

Not to mention, we were still harboring a big secret. The pandemic had forced us to stick close to home for the better part of a year now. Outside of our care team, we might as well have been invisible. That meant Soraya's worsening condition had been easy to hide.

But minus a much hoped for reprieve from the NIH, staying silent didn't feel like an option anymore. So, I took to our blog, wrote a heartfelt message, and hit publish. I understood the news might come as a surprise to even our closest family and friends, but I also recognized that pretending things were different wasn't healthy for any of us.

My post read:

Over the past several months Soraya's health has been declining.

We were grateful for the opportunity to have been at the National Institutes of Health last week. Going five hundred miles for more insight, more hope, really puts things in perspective. To be surrounded by families and children with rare life-threatening diseases was overwhelming, but to have the realization that we are now a part of this club is devastating.

For a time when people are questioning science, here we are as a family praying for science to prolong Soraya's life and improve her quality of life. This is the only hope we have left.

She's getting more tired, losing strength in the muscles, and has a ventilator at night.

She decided it was time for her to start using a wheelchair regularly.

While Soraya's physical strength dwindles, her inner strength shines. This girl did every test and every procedure without hesitation. Her motivation was to "have the doctors figure out what is happening to my body" and "get back home to my sisters."

As a family we hope her decline plateaus for a bit so we can continue to suck the joy out of life. We've done it all, we still do it all. New exomes, new genomes. The NIH in Bethesda, Maryland, is actively still working on

Soraya's case. They're actually right now re-analyzing Soraya's muscle biopsy from the past.

No, we haven't given up. We just know we're out of options.

I was humbled by the immediate and overwhelming response. It somehow came as news to me that we did not have to bear this alone—people wanted to help us carry the heavy emotional burden. Unfortunately, this realization didn't come with an instruction manual, and I still needed to learn how to let people in again after so fiercely protecting our privacy for so long.

Amidst our sorrow came a bright light: Make-A-Wish stepped up and generously offered to grant Soraya's wish. After much deliberation—and a few disappointments, like the Nickelodeon resort in Punta Cana not being an option—she made her choice of surfing in Hawaii. It was an unsurprising decision. Ever since she was a little girl, Soraya has always loved being in the water—she's a total fish.

Still, this added yet another layer of fear that made truly sucking the joy out of life difficult. The previous month, the girls had been catching waves in Lake Michigan when Soraya started shaking and feeling like she was going to pass out. I grabbed her out of the water and took her heart rate. It was in the 180s. Typically, it should be about one-third of that.

We wrapped her up, took her back to the rental house, and measured her blood sugar. It registered a 32, and the normal range is between 70 and 100. Once we gave her juice, the level went up— but then it dipped right back down again. This up-and-down cycle continued for two full weeks, during which time we needed to add cornstarch, a slow-moving carb, to her G-tube feedings to hold her steady.

And now she wanted to surf. In the ocean waves. In Hawaii.

177

Good Life

Historically, we knew any kind of exercise—which for Soraya could now mean walking half a block, dancing for five minutes, or body surfing a wave or two—was often enough to drop her blood sugar for at least a few days. If it went too low, the condition could become life-threatening, leading to seizures, brain damage, diabetic ketoacidosis, and even death. We needed a plan in case she had the same kind of reaction on her wish trip.

We had Soraya admitted to the hospital for a hypoglycemic challenge. She knew what and why we were doing this and was very agreeable to it. None of us wanted to revisit the Lake Michigan debacle again, most especially Soraya.

During the test, the medical team eventually got her blood sugar down to 50, then ran labs to determine why her body could not fully stabilize itself. As with everything about Soraya's case, no culprit could be found. Other than her blood sugar, all the tests came back normal.

This meant food was the only treatment option available. As we already had been doing, doctors recommended juice as our first line of defense. If that failed and Soraya became unresponsive, we were given glucose gel to squirt in her mouth. Our care team was honest, telling us they had no idea if it would work and that it was simply their best guess.

Even though we were told it was safe for us to travel to Hawaii, I insisted on an emergency plan and researched nearby hospitals. Of course I wanted Soraya to have this experience, but I also felt like I needed to be proactive and prepared. We had never flown with her ventilator before, and it felt like a big stretch. There were so many things to consider, like making sure there was an outlet nearby and enough battery to power it at higher elevations.

As we were trying to get a handle on the more logistical pieces of the Make-A-Wish trip, one of Safi's best friends let us know he wanted to be there to support us. "As much as this is going to be a beautiful experience, I'm sure there are also going to be really hard moments," he told Safi. "I want to be your person during those." We were thrilled by his kindness and accepted his offer readily. After that, a beautiful cascade of friends and family decided they wanted to come witness. Eventually, our group grew to include 16 special people in our lives.

We made sure everyone knew this was not going to be a jam-packed itinerary type of celebration because Soraya's depleted energy levels wouldn't allow for it. The surfing lesson was the main event, plus a luau one night. The rest of the time, we planned to do nothing at all, except for group dinners. Everyone said they wanted to join us anyway, and we felt incredibly humbled by and grateful for their love and support.

Soraya positively glowed under the love of her extended family and friends, as did all of us. Their presence made the entire trip feel like magic and a giant reprieve from the relentless daily struggles we were so accustomed to.

When the day came for the surfing lesson, we dove into it as a family. Safi and I were terrified, but the girls—and most especially Soraya—absolutely loved it. On the board, her face registered pure joy. She seemed free of the physical limitations that had been placed on her body. Seeing her fearlessly conquer the waves choked every-one up, and soon we were all crying tears of happiness intermingled with the deep sadness of knowing she'd never be physically strong enough to do this again.

And in that moment, *suck the joy out of life* took on a life of its own for the Faruqui Five, as we were now calling ourselves. It became permanently imprinted in our minds. It began singing in our hearts: *We must grab joy while we can. We must go and get it. Time is getting shorter.*

Personal insight: Our Make-A-Wish trip taught us to face our fears of traveling with Soraya's medical equipment. Not only did we ride on a plane we rode *waves*. Our fears and attempts at blaming logistics created a narrative for all that we couldn't do. We just needed Make-A-Wish to truly show us how with a bit of creativity and tremendous support, we could make anything happen. This has been our greatest family lesson.

Universal takeaway: You guessed it! Suck the joy out of life. We must be intentional and actively grab joy while we can. We must go and get it . . . and not wait for it.

Chapter 26

Home

One thing Safi and I said we'd never do as parents was get a pet, no matter how much our kids begged us. Not even a fish. But life has a funny way of changing those "nevers" into "okay, fine."

We'd already gotten our first cat a few years back, not understanding that the feline persuasion doesn't necessarily want to be snuggled all day—which was what we hoped Prince would do with Soraya when we welcomed him into our family. Wrong! He immediately took to Yasmeen and never gave the rest of us a second glance.

While planning for the Make-A-Wish trip, Soraya made it known that she wanted her own cat. Worried that a new pet would choose someone else as their favorite again, I concocted a story about how *I* had been thinking about asking for a cat for Mother's Day. My thought was if this one failed to bond with Soraya, she wouldn't be as upset as if it had been chosen just for her.

My suggestion was met with great enthusiasm. I called a breeder, put down a deposit, and sealed the deal. We decided to call this new kitty Ohana, which is Hawaiian for family, and even bestowed her with a middle name—Kiki—after Waikiki Beach, our home away from home during the Wish trip.

When we picked up "my" gorgeous new kitty after Hawaii, she made a beeline straight for Soraya. Phew. Safi and I heaved a big sigh of relief—until Leena started a campaign for her own pet: a dog. We managed to stave her off for a time, but eventually, we'd go from our no-pets rule to three-pet home, from never to a menagerie.

One day soon after our trip, Soraya was cuddling with Ohana as I was giving her a massage. I realized she was more relaxed than I'd seen her in quite a while, so I decided to ask palliative care how to find a qualified massage therapist for her. It seemed like it would be a great adjunct to her ever-increasing need for pain meds.

Palliative care told me I could either look for a licensed therapist on my own or simply use the service available through their hospice team. When I remarked that we were not in hospice, Dr. Meyer told me nonchalantly, "Oh, that's not a problem. I can change your status to palliative care *and* hospice. That way, you'll still have access to me for pain control, but you'll also get additional home health resources like massage therapy, child life services, and music therapy for Soraya and her siblings."

We simply had to agree to a nurse visiting our home every two months to establish and maintain eligibility. It was a no-brainer.

Just as quickly, though, I spiraled into the same kind of overthinking that had accompanied asking for palliative care. *Oh, boy, did I do it again? Did I manifest something bad here? Is this Dr. Meyer's way of introducing hospice to us in the gentlest way possible?* The only thing I knew for sure was that I trusted him completely by now, so I went ahead with it.

Still, joining Starshine Hospice felt like leaping into an entirely different reality. While I knew hospice doesn't equate to imminent death in pediatrics, it does acknowledge an irreversible, steady decline in a child's health. I wanted to protect all my children from this knowledge as long as possible and even went so far as to hide the binder the nurse gave us during her first visit because I didn't want them to see the word *hospice*. My feeling at the time was that it was unfair to expect any child, especially one with special needs, to regularly contemplate their mortality.

As with palliative care, I went in thinking we'd use it for that one service but soon came to find there were many more benefits we wanted to take them up on. Soraya loved massage therapy, and the girls loved doing music therapy together. It was a great fit for our family.

And, when the nurse mentioned we'd have a discussion every two years about whether it made sense to remain in hospice, I saw it as a small ray of hope.

Still, I knew it was beyond a long shot. Things were already happening far faster than the 10-year stabilization our care team had floated less than a year ago. Soraya was now not only using the ventilator all night, but she had started needing increasingly longer windows during the day. I felt the tracheostomy talk looming ever closer.

In anticipation of needing to give Soraya this news, Safi and I arranged for Leena and Yasmeen to learn about it from palliative care. We felt it was important for the rest of the family to be in alignment so we'd be able to support Soraya once she was given the information. I asked a child life specialist we'd been working with since Soraya was three to help Dr. Meyer deliver the message in an age-appropriate way. She prepared visuals so the girls could envision how a tracheostomy works.

It was a divide-and-conquer maneuver. I attended the meeting with Leena and Safi went with Yasmeen. Leena's questions were very equipment-specific and practical in nature.

"How does this work?"

"How can you tell if it's broken?"

"Do you think my sister will still be able to swim?" (The answer was probably not.)

"Wait, do you think she's getting too tired to swim?" (Probably yes.)

When all those were answered, she was satisfied and accepting of the procedure. In essence, she seemed to feel like "Okay, cool. That can help Soraya."

On the other end of the spectrum was Yasmeen. She became hysterical when she learned what was happening and absolutely drilled into Dr. Meyer.

"What if Soraya doesn't want that? What will that mean?"

"What if she *does* want it? What will that mean?"

"Do you really not know what's happening to her?"

"What's the prognosis?"

"What do you mean, you don't have a prognosis? Give me a timeline."

Backed against the wall by my precocious preteen, Dr. Meyer said that he didn't have a crystal ball, but he estimated that Soraya had one to two years left to live. He hadn't shared this kind of information with our family before, probably because we'd never asked before. I'd always assumed he'd wait until it was time, which I now could only suppose had come.

I respected that Dr. Meyer had been fully transparent with her. It earned him—and us—a lot of trust. Yasmeen now understood without a doubt no one was hiding anything from her. It didn't make the reality any less harsh, but it soothed the hypervigilant part of her brain that was always searching for hidden information.

Still, my heart wept for Yasmeen. Once again, she'd been put in a very unfair, very adult position. She couldn't unhear the news, and it haunted her. Absolutely devastated, Safi vacillated between righteous anger and the deepest sorrow. And even though I'd intuitively known in my heart this was happening, hearing it spoken into reality was absolutely soul-crushing.

Our worst fears were coming true.

Personal insight: We said we'd *never* have any pets. We ended up with three within three years and they have been such a gift. They have provided love, comfort, and humor. I had no idea what I was missing out on. I am grateful for our persistent children to soften us.

Universal takeaway: Never say never or have absolutes in your family. You never know how life circumstances will change you. If you're open to it, you may allow a great love or extraordinary experience that you would have never gotten otherwise.

Chapter 27

Pompeii

On top of everything else, Soraya's baby teeth refused to fall out, and now her adult teeth were trying to crowd their way into her mouth, too. Not only was it painful, but it put her at a big risk for infection. That left us with no choice. Soraya needed 10 teeth pulled, and it had to be done in the hospital because anesthesia had such an adverse effect on her.

Whenever Soraya has surgery, it's a three-day affair. We have to get to the hospital the night before for monitoring and stay an extra night to ensure her heart rate is steady and she doesn't go into shock. It's always stressful, made even more so this time because the procedure was scheduled during the week of Yasmeen's 13th birthday.

Trying to balance Soraya's medical needs while simultaneously making sure Leena and Yasmeen feel equally valued and loved isn't easy. I try but I don't always succeed. Leena recently expressed to me that she feels like Barbie's shoe, a mere accessory to Soraya. Yasmeen puts it this way: "Soraya is the sun and we're just planets orbiting her."

The surgery went well, but the second we got home, our nanny asked to speak with me. She told me through her tears, "Ohana has a rare disease called feline intestinal peritonitis, or FIP. You have to call the vet today to let her know whether you want to try an experimental drug or put her to sleep."

While Safi and I had been busy at the hospital with Soraya, she'd taken Ohana to the vet for us. We'd only had Ohana for a month and she was sneezing a lot, so we wanted to know if it was due to allergies, a kitty cold, or something else. What an irony that now even our cat had a rare, life-threatening illness.

"I don't even know why I'm so upset," the nanny told me. "I think it must be because Ohana represents Soraya to me."

I dropped my luggage, pulled our nanny into a hug, and started crying with her. I had no idea what to do in the face of this latest crisis. I needed to talk to Safi, who is a rock in every situation but especially when it comes to hard decisions like this one.

I called Safi and gave him the lowdown. Instead of holding strong like usual, he totally lost it. "I just can't do it," he said, meaning put Ohana down. "It feels like this cat is Soraya. If this were her, we'd try the medicine."

His response was not at all what I'd been expecting, but I understood completely. Everyone was connecting the dots between Soraya's and Ohana's conditions. That cat truly was Soraya's in every way, even down to her health status.

Between the hospital time and the cat's illness, I was completely exhausted from the odyssey of the last three days. I was just about to change into sweats and collapse on the couch when Safi got an unexpected phone call. He ushered me into the kitchen and whispered, "I'm pretty sure you're going to say no, but I put our name on the cancellation list for the Andy Grammer concert tonight. They have two tickets available."

Andy is one of Yasmeen's favorite musicians. I'd wanted to get tickets to celebrate her birthday, but the show was sold out and I hadn't been able to find affordable resale tickets to the event. It was now five in the evening and the show started in an hour and a half. I hadn't slept for days, and I was an emotional wreck. But it was

Yasmeen's birthday, and I didn't want her to feel like an orbiting planet as always.

"You know what," I said, gathering up all my reserves. "Yasmeen deserves this. We're going."

I went back out into the den and whispered the big news in Yasmeen's ear. Thrilled, she went to change while I called an Uber. I was so overwrought that I didn't trust myself to drive us there safely. I looked over at Safi. "You think you can handle Ohana's experimental medication by yourself? It is an injection, you know."

He assured me he was up for the challenge even though he'd never injected a cat before. I certainly hadn't either. We were just going to have to wing it. "May the force be with you," I told him as Yasmeen and I were leaving. "You got this."

At the concert, I was astonished to learn Yasmeen knew every song by heart. I was only familiar with the ones that had been on the radio, but I quickly figured out why she was such a big fan: Andy sings about the beautiful things in life—like his daughter being born—as well as the hard things, like his mom dying. Each provided a beautiful emotional release.

Yasmeen and I became our very own solar system at that moment, orbiting each other in tentative circles. Temporarily removed from the burning white light of Soraya's sun, we danced and cried out into the night. Left to our own devices, we shed enough tears to fill the salty oceans of Jupiter's largest moon.

Personal insight: The Andy Grammer concert was a beautiful reminder on how much music can create connection, provide an emotional outlet, and create hope. It also provided a way for Yasmeen and me to connect without words. We could sing at the top of our lungs, cry, and hold each other.

It had been so long since I turned to music to help me cope with life, and this was another turning point in putting this in our family tool kit for life. More specifically, hearing the way that Andy sang of grief, joy, and love created a deep personal connection for me. It resonated with my emotions and echoed some of our current experiences.

Universal takeaway: Music has the power to transcend all languages, speaking directly to the heart in a way words alone never could.

Chapter 28

Riptide

Now that the rest of the family was informed and prepared, both we and our palliative care team felt it was time to discuss the tracheostomy with Soraya. This sparked a lot of hard conversations. Safi and I needed to be on the same page about the trach before we met with Soraya, and we weren't yet in agreement about how we felt.

Even though I'm a pediatrician, I'd recently learned some new information about the procedure that gave me pause. For starters, it would involve a minimum six-week stay in the hospital, which would more than likely turn into three months. The stoma (hole through which the tube is placed) needed to heal, a trach change would need to be performed, and at-home nursing care would have to be secured before discharge. In my opinion, that was already a deal breaker.

Then there was the fact that the nursing care necessary for trach patients is a 24-hour endeavor. Because trachs can be dislodged at any time, someone would always have to be awake and watching Soraya while she slept. This requirement is not temporary, it's forever.

What's more, this invasion of privacy wouldn't just be at home, it would be everywhere. Even in the car. At any point, a mucus plug could form, so we'd need a nurse riding in the back seat with Soraya anytime we drove somewhere.

At the time, it was often thought that people with trachs can't have pets. What would we do with our two cats, one of which we'd spent an insane amount of money saving from imminent death? The girls would be devastated.

And how about the fact that Soraya would never be able to go swimming again? My little fish, banished to land for the rest of her life. Just the thought of it broke my heart. How much can one child be expected to lose?

The medical risks haunted me as well. There can be complications from getting a trach inserted. There's always the possibility it will fall out. Every six months, Soraya would have to have it scoped in the hospital. Because of her blood sugar and anesthesia difficulties, that meant she'd spend at least three days out of every six months in the intensive care unit (ICU).

Of course I wanted Soraya to live longer, but what kind of life would that be? Because breathing difficulties were only one of her many symptoms, it wouldn't be a lifesaving procedure, only a life-extending one—who knows for how long, and with many restrictions. I didn't want a nurse living in our home. I didn't want someone in the back seat every time we went for a drive. I was looking for a better quality of life not only for Soraya but our entire family.

Safi didn't like those aspects of getting the tracheostomy any more than I did, but he simply couldn't fathom *not* doing it. "What's our alternative?" he asked with tears in his eyes. "I'm not ready to let her go. Our family has resources. We can do this."

We even tossed around the idea of me quitting my job to cover more of Soraya's medical care, but I felt the cost to both me and our family would be too great. I was already stretched so thin. I truly believed I might snap under the added pressure.

"At what point would you allow Soraya *not* to have a trach?" I asked Safi.

"Only if that's really what she wanted," he replied. "I couldn't look her in the eye and make her go through that otherwise."

He asked me the same question in reverse. "At what point would you *allow* her to get a trach?"

"If she understood all of the implications and risks and still wanted to be here longer, I would muster up the courage to do it," I told him.

"Do you really think she has the ability to decide something like this for herself?" he mused, still pondering both sides of the argument.

"We've been telling her what to do for the past 10 years," I said, discovering I had even stronger feelings on the subject than I'd realized. "We've taken her to too many doctor's appointments and therapy sessions to even count, and we never once asked her opinion. Maybe the payoff for that now is that she gets to make this decision for herself. At this point, I think she deserves to have a say in what her life looks like."

Looking at the situation through a lens of autonomy, we both agreed Soraya should get to decide whether a tracheostomy was something she wanted. Once she understood both sides of the argument, we'd let the chips fall where they may. It was her decision now.

Dr. Meyer and a child life specialist who knows our family well agreed to take the lead. They left it up to us whether we wanted to be in the room during the discussion and we chose not to. We felt Soraya would be able to read our emotions, and we wanted her to make her decision without worrying about its impact on us.

In that meeting, Dr. Meyer presented the information to Soraya in a very factual manner appropriate for her maturity and level of understanding. He offered her several bullet points on each side of the coin: what it would be like to have a trach, and what it would be like to not have one.

He let her know a tracheostomy could prolong her life, but he did not attach a timeline to it. I was grateful for this omission, because I would hate for Soraya to pick something out of pure fear. Let's face it, we're all scared of dying. If Dr. Meyer had said, "Either you get this trach or you die," I'm sure she would have decided to get it on the spot. Instead, he presented her options in an honest, measured way, and for that I'll be forever grateful.

The bullet points he presented Soraya about having a tracheostomy were these:

- It would require surgery and being in the hospital for six weeks to three months.
- There would be routine hospitalizations that meant she'd be in the ICU for about a week every year.
- She would never be able to swim again.
- There would be a high chance of her losing her voice or having it sound different.
- She would live a longer life.

And the bullet points about not getting a trach were these:

- She would keep her voice.
- She would live how she is living now.
- She would need her ventilator more and more.
- She would not live as long.

After giving her all the options, Dr. Meyer left Soraya alone to process the information and consider her decision. I was so anxious she would say she wanted a trach, and I'm sure Safi was worried she'd say she didn't want one. In less than 10 minutes, she'd made her choice: No trach.

She told us the biggest reason was that she didn't want to lose her voice—she wanted to make an impact on the world and couldn't envision doing so without the ability to speak. Not being able to swim ran a close second. She also did not want to spend all that time in the hospital away from family or always have someone with her in her room and the car.

"Are you sure?" we asked her.

She said she was positive and didn't want to talk about it any further. She's very decisive, and her choice was final.

On the car ride home, Soraya piped up from the back seat. "This is like an unfair *would you rather* game. Both choices are bad. Either I get a thing in my neck and lose my voice and not be able to swim or I live how I want to live but don't get to live as long. Why can't there be any other option?"

"I wish there were," I told her. "That wasn't an easy decision."

"Well, I want to live how I want to live," she declared.

If the only gift we could give her after 10 years of surgeries, tests, doctor's visits, and therapies was her own voice, then that's exactly what we were going to do. It was her life. She had every right to go through it the way she wanted to.

We all want to live according to our own internal guidance. This was hers, so we needed to be willing to accept it.

Personal insight: The deliberation between Safi and me over Soraya getting a trach really showed our differences in opinions. The biggest revelation we had was that Soraya should have a choice. As parents we knew that she was capable of doing this with proper guidance and checking for understanding.

Universal takeaway: There's no greater gift than having the ability to make decisions for yourself and your health . . . even if you are a child.

Chapter 29

Don't Give Up on Me

We're big on dance parties in our family, and by now Andy Grammer's music punctuated our favorite playlists. When he was announced as the performer for Cincinnati Children's annual fundraiser, we couldn't believe our luck. I scored second-row seats the day tickets went on sale.

Every month, the girls worked on a group activity together with Starshine Hospice. Once they knew about going to see Andy in concert, they decided to make a video for him as their project. Wearing *suck the joy out of life* jerseys, they told him how much they loved his music and thanked him for coming to raise money for the hospital. Starshine said they'd try to get the finished piece to Andy but couldn't guarantee anything.

The week before the show, we found out there was going to be a meet and greet earlier in the day before the fundraiser. Even better, we were 1 of 10 families invited to it. Everyone was so excited to be included.

At the meet and greet, Yasmeen walked right up to Andy and explained how much his honest, raw lyrics resonated with her. "The song about your mom when she passed away really connects with me because my sister is progressing." I saw his eyes change as he realized both our situation and that Yasmeen was a true fan. Soraya hugged him and asked if he had gotten their video. He said yes, and she broke into a giant smile.

He proceeded to play a couple of songs for the group. Yasmeen was singing along at the top of her lungs. At one point, he stopped and exclaimed, "Wow, you've got a voice!" She was ecstatic.

After I took the kids back to school, I got a call telling me Andy wanted our girls to sing with him onstage during the concert. "Do you think they'd be comfortable with that?"

"No, they'll be freaking out," I replied. "But I'm not going to tell them until right before they go on, and they'll be great." Because it would have been too difficult to get Soraya backstage from the seats we had purchased, they moved us to box seats. An even better score!

When I told the girls the big news, they started screaming and jumping around. I thought they might be nervous, but when I told them the song they'd be performing was "Don't Give Up on Me," they had total confidence. It was already a crowd favorite in our house and everyone knew the words by heart. The lyrics were so fitting to our situation:

I'm not givin' up, givin' up
No not me
Even when nobody else believes
I'm not goin' down that easily
So don't give up on me
I will fight
I will fight for you
I always do until my heart
Is black and blue

The Faruqui Five enjoyed the first part of the performance from our fancy box seats, all of us singing along and rocking out. At the appointed time, our nanny took the girls backstage so Safi and I could stay in the audience and watch them perform. They totally nailed it, and we of course ended up in a puddle of tears.

But even though Yasmeen had alluded to Soraya's declining condition during the meet and greet with Andy, no one outside of her, Safi, and me was aware of the timeline Dr. Meyer had given yet. I was starting to wonder if it was fair to keep it a secret, especially from Soraya. I didn't like that we were picking and choosing what she did and didn't know about her condition.

I kept asking Dr. Meyer, "When do we tell her?" His guidance was always "She'll ask when she wants to know—and by the time she asks, she'll probably already know."

Lately, Soraya had been wondering more about her medications and equipment. "Is this helping me? Is this making me better?"

My standard answer was "Your body's getting weaker, and we're doing the best we can."

"Well, what's going to help it then?"

"We don't know."

Soon, the timeline started feeling like a ticking bomb. I wanted to tell our families the truth, but I didn't want everyone to start a countdown once we did. *One year until Soraya dies. Six months until she passes. Seven weeks until she's gone.* And, if we told our families, that meant I would have to share the news with Soraya—and I was terrified about how she'd take the news.

Soraya solved the quandary for us on Thanksgiving. "I want you and Dad to tell me everything you know about my condition."

My heart started racing. I'd known this day would come eventually, but I still wasn't prepared now that it was in front of me. "What do you mean?" I asked, stalling.

"I want you to tell me everything that's happening with my body," she replied. "I'm interested in what the doctors say about me."

Safi and I gave each other a pained look. As I was gathering my thoughts and searching for a way to begin the conversation, Soraya offered us a short reprieve. "Actually, save it for Christmas. I want it to be a special day."

199

Don't Give Up on Me

That gave us a month to prepare, so we consulted with Dr. Meyer and her therapist Dr. Aimee. Their advice was to wait for Soraya to ask specific questions, answer those directly, and be as honest and factual as possible. "Don't use words like *go to sleep* or *pass away*, Dr. Meyer told us. "Say *die*. Say the word."

Christmas came and before we even got to the presents, Soraya asked when we were going to have the talk. We told her we wanted to enjoy opening gifts first. I was dreading the whole thing.

After the last piece of wrapping paper had been ripped and the last present had been opened, Safi and I took Soraya into our room. We all sat down on the bed and stared at each other. Awkward silence took over.

"Okay, go," Soraya prompted us.

Following the advice given, I said, "Ask me a specific question."

Soraya gave me a bemused look. "Mom, you know my brain can't think like that."

Here we go, I thought. Taking a deep breath, I dove in. "Okay, well, you know you have a medical condition, and no one can figure out what it is . . ."

"Yes, I know that."

"And that your body's getting tired."

"I know that, too, Mom."

"And the truth is, it's going to continue to get tired, and there's nothing that we can do to stop it."

Soraya got very quiet. "Well, what exactly is going to get tired?"

"Your muscles are going to continue to get tired. Your breathing muscles are getting tired from breathing, so that's why you have your machine."

She took that information in. "So is my machine helping me?" It was not the first time she'd asked this question. I think she kept hoping for a different answer.

200

Keep Your Head Up

"It's helping you breathe really well while you use it, but when you don't use it, it's not helpful. Your muscles are getting weaker and weaker, and when your muscles aren't working as well, you can get sick really easily. That's why we're so concerned about COVID and why we're wearing masks. And that's pretty much it."

She shook her head. I really hadn't told her anything new, and she was still looking for information. "Tell me the rest. I told you. I want to know everything."

Safi stared at me, imploring me to leave the conversation where it was. It had gone so well. But she was asking for something more and I felt like she deserved our honesty.

"The thing is when your body gets weaker, it will make it harder for you to breathe. And when you're not able to breathe, it will mean that your heart muscle stops working and you won't be able to live."

"Wait. What?! I'm dying?!" Soraya wailed. I'd put faith in Dr. Meyer's experience that most children know the truth by the time they ask, but this wasn't the case with Soraya. She was totally caught off guard by the information.

My mind started racing. *Oh no! What have I done? Can I take it back?!* I had to fight myself from trying to retract the words and say, *No, no, no, it's fine. Everything's fine.* Because it wasn't fine, and I didn't want to take it back. I'd finally exposed the truth, and there was a lot of relief in that.

I avoided looking at Safi's eyes but still caught a glimpse of utter sadness. Not at me, but at the situation. We held Soraya as she sobbed.

"I'm confused. I don't understand. I'm dying? I don't want to die!"

I moved the hair out of her face and explained that the doctors had no idea when she would die, just like none of us know when we will die. "As the time gets closer, I promise we'll let you know," I told her.

201

Don't Give Up on Me

"I don't want to die. I want to stay," she said through her tears. "I'm mad at God. Why would he choose this for me?! What's our plan B? Should I get the trach? No. I need a plan that's easier than that!"

Safi and I told Soraya that she's an angel on earth. We explained that God loves her very much and would always take care of her. This wasn't just lip service—we genuinely believe she has a special connection to God and his angels.

Suddenly, her expression changed. She jumped up out of bed and declared, "I need to tell my sisters!"

"Why don't we wait until after the New Year for that?" I suggested. We had preemptively set up a meeting with Yasmeen and Leena in January and were hoping to enjoy the rest of the holiday as a family without dwelling on death. That was not an option for Soraya.

She was firm. "No, these are my sisters. I need to tell them."

Once the girls were gathered in the room with us, Soraya announced, "The doctors have been talking. They know my body is getting weaker, and I'm going to be dying sooner. And that's the news that I need to tell you."

Leena looked incredibly stoic. A single tear rolled down her face, seemingly in slow motion. "Soraya, I've known," she admitted.

I said, "Leena, how did you know?"

"Mom, I put it together," she said, more tears flowing now. "When people get older, they get weaker and then sometimes they need wheelchairs and things to help them breathe. I saw that happening with Soraya, and that's why I never wanted to talk about it. I knew what it all meant."

The Faruqui Five held each other and cried for what seemed like an eternity. Then, Soraya took it upon herself to make us all feel better by telling us jokes. She gave everyone a hug and a snuggle.

"Just so you know, I'm not scared of dying," she stated matter-of-factly. I'm sure it was a sentiment meant to comfort us, her family,

202

Keep Your Head Up

more than the reality of the situation. Still, I was in awe of her grace under pressure.

"It's okay if you are," I told her. "Most people are."

"It's like I have cancer, but I get to keep my hair," Soraya mused. "Wait, I *do* get to keep my hair, right?"

We all started laughing through our tears. Isn't it funny, how joy can still be found in our very worst moments of pain? How hope always finds its way through whatever small crevice is available?

Personal insight: Our palliative care physician was correct; Soraya would ask about her health when she wanted to know. As for Leena, I was shocked at how much she had picked up on from pure observation. Despite how hard that conversation was, there was a weight lifted from all. The release came from speaking the words, acknowledging it, and crying together.

Universal takeaway: Hard conversations are made easier by actually having the conversation, being honest, and being with others. Sharing the weight and being a witness helps so much. A shared experience is lighter.

Chapter 30

Time of Your Life

Now that the elephant in the room had been acknowledged, we could all breathe freely. We knew whatever happened from here on out would be a shared experience, and we were in it to win it. *Suck the Joy Out of Life* came online at full force.

We dubbed 2023 the Year of Yes. Safi and I had been saving money for a rainy day—a medical emergency or when time was running out. We suddenly understood, *This is exactly what we've been preparing for. Let's go make the best memories.*

I didn't think we'd consider another big trip after Make a Wish, but its success gave us the bravery to push onward. We knew Soraya's energy wouldn't be able to support these larger experiences for much longer. We were determined to soak it all in.

We went to Disney World and Universal. Per Leena's request, we swam with the dolphins. Soraya's choices were the Lilo and Stitch restaurant and the Harry Potter exhibit. She was dead set on getting a wand and going shopping. We did the VIP experience for all of it, since we knew this could be our last time here. But that really goes for anyone, doesn't it? None of us know when our "lasts" are except in hindsight.

Next, we got to watch the Cincinnati Bengals from a suite, go down on the field, and get a signed Joe Burrow jersey. This was a year they went to the Super Bowl, so it was extra exciting. The girls decided football was more fun than they'd realized.

We were also lucky enough to secure excellent seats for the Taylor Swift Eras concert. Because the show was a three-hour-plus marathon, having a suite was essential for Soraya's comfort. We needed to ensure she had close access to a restroom and ample space for her medication and sip ventilator.

All the Faruqui girls and a couple of our Swifty caregivers went to the show. Safi opted out so he could be our much-needed Uber driver, whom we lovingly named Joe. Like so many people that summer, we spent months deciding on the outfits from the different Eras, listening to Taylor on repeat, and making many, many bracelets.

As a family, we'd already started the practice of making bucket lists, but now we decided to dive into it deeper. It wasn't about doing more expensive things but pursuing the things we love most. Sometimes these experiences overlapped, and we did them as a family, like when Yasmeen wished to make s'mores by a campfire. Other times, they were geared specifically to one person, like Yasmeen's request to go on a mother-daughter trip to touch the ocean or Leena's desire to get a dog—which Safi finally relented to, bringing Taco the white golden retriever into our lives.

Music has always been the heartbeat of the Faruqui Five, and we all have deep connections to songs. Long before I was in conventional therapy, music was my therapy. Since music and dancing are our jam, it's unsurprising that many of our bucket list items revolved around going to concerts.

Yasmeen and I saw P!nk together, and Yasmeen and Safi saw NF. Safi, Leena, and Yasmeen saw Rüfüs Du Sol, and Safi and I saw U2 at the Sphere in Las Vegas. Leena has recently put in a request to see her favorite performer, Olivia Rodrigo.

And then guess who we all got to see again? Andy Grammer. Every one of us had become true fans. The girls love him even more than Taylor Swift, which I know is really hard to imagine.

There wasn't a meet and greet scheduled for this particular concert, but I kept checking the website in case one became available. Magically, 48 hours before the show, I saw a VIP upgrade option on the website. I snagged 8 of the available 12 tickets for our family and caregivers.

As part of the meet and greet experience, we were invited onto Andy's tour bus. Soraya parked her wheelchair next to him and asked, "Where are you sitting?" He told her, "Wherever you are!" Soraya was absolutely delighted when he plunked himself right down next to her.

"I want to go around and have everyone talk about the last time you really felt loved," Andy told us once everyone was settled in.

Soraya said, "Any day with my family." I cited Soraya's recent choir concert where 18 people—most of them not even relatives—came to watch her perform. Leena named the day Safi said we could get Taco, and Yasmeen said while she tries hard to not feel loved, she can't help but feel loved because we're always loving on her. It was such a Yasmeen comment to make.

Next, Andy asked Soraya, "What's your favorite song?"

"You know my favorite song," she replied, all smiles. "It's the one we sang together onstage!"

He grinned back at her. "Okay, do you want to sing with me, or do you want me to sing to you?"

"Either way," Soraya said with a shrug, just happy to be experiencing it all.

Andy belted out the first couple of words and then Yasmeen joined in. "I love the way that sounds," he told her. She could not have been more excited.

Still, after the meet and greet was over, Yasmeen admitted, "I know I need to be happy right now, but I just can't be. Nothing and everything is wrong."

"Just let it be," I told her. "Feel whatever you need to feel."

207

Time of Your Life

During the concert, we sang along to every song, alternately crying and laughing. Right before the end of the show, Andy announced, "I want to dedicate 'Don't Give Up on Me' to a girl named Soraya. We don't know how long she has to live, but tonight we want her to feel loved." We could not believe our ears—in that moment, every single person in the crowd was singing directly to her. Joy was somehow once again arising out of pain. I don't know why it surprises me every time how comfortably those two can coexist.

At the end of the show, there were fireworks. One of Soraya's biggest fears is loud noises, so she had never seen them before. This time, though, we'd brought along her sensory headphones. The look on her face as she watched the colorful explosions in the sky for the first time—right after having an entire amphitheater of people sing to her—was priceless. People from all around stopped to give us words of encouragement. The kindness just didn't stop.

We were going big, really fast. The highs were so high that it got increasingly difficult to settle into the lowest of lows that inevitably followed. The roller coaster had to stop at some point, but until then we were hurtling through space and time with joyful abandon.

Personal insight: Creating bucket lists and then fulfilling dreams were a salve for the pain. They were reminders of how good life can be.

Universal takeaway: Make a bucket list, prioritize it, and create time. Don't wait. Just do it.

Chapter 31

Landslide

While sucking the joy out of life often seemed attainable during an incredible concert or other bucket list experience, anticipatory grief was its omnipresent partner. It cloaked daily life in a dark, foreboding cloud, the associated depression, fear, and worry weighing heavily on us all. And the worst part was, we couldn't outrun it.

There had already been so many losses. Soraya was no longer able to do any of her therapies—which had allowed her to grow and thrive—because she was too tired, so we had to say goodbye to many beloved caregivers. She had gone from full days at school to half days to an hour and a half a day. The best we could hope for in the upcoming year was continuing this very limited schedule, and the worst-case scenario was no school at all.

Dance parties had become fewer and farther in between. When the kids were younger, we danced after every meal. Now, with the right songs, I could still sometimes get Soraya to dance with us. Her eyes would light up and she'd tell me, "Mom, this is worth it." Afterwards, she'd be tired for the rest of the day, but the glimmer was still there.

Big trips had turned into staycations had turned into mini trips to Starbucks or Ulta at the mall. Swimming wasn't an option for my little fish anymore. Really, anything that involved more than a couch and a screen had become increasingly difficult to manage.

Soraya now had a sip ventilator to support her ventilation needs in between regular ventilator windows. Opioid patches had replaced weaker pain medications, in ever-increasing dosages. Bedtime had been permanently moved to what used to be dinnertime. The changes just keep on coming, and we all manage our feelings about the ever-evolving situation differently.

As when Soraya was first born and we were desperately looking for answers about her condition, Safi and I still take turns falling apart. There is a natural ebb and flow to our emotions that serves us well. There are certain situations I know I can hold it together for, and others where he can but I can't. We know how fortunate we are to operate this way and are grateful we don't actively feel the same things at the same time.

Safi can start crying at any second, without warning. I know I'm lucky to have a partner who's not shoving away his feelings, but there was a time when he wanted to talk about Soraya's impending death every night right before bed. "What do you think her funeral is going to be like? Who do you think will come? How will the burial happen?"

"I love you, but this is why you have a therapist," I told him. "I can't go down to that deep, dark place with you. If I try to meet you where you're at right now, I don't think I'll be able to get myself back up to keep this household going."

Now he tries to stop himself. If it's right before bed and I ask, "What's on your mind?" he'll say, "You don't want to know." He writes his feelings down and we talk about them during the day, when I won't perseverate on the conversation or lose quite as much sleep over it. I can acknowledge his feelings, I can see that he's hurting, and I'm also fully aware we process very differently.

Because for me, I only allow myself to cry when no one else is upset. If everything's good, that's the only time it feels safe for me to express my grief. Safi often worries that I'm bottling everything up.

Once, he said to me, "I need you to go somewhere to release your feelings," so I went to a hotel and tried to manufacture a sob session by watching sad movies and thinking about death. It didn't happen.

Instead, grief comes to me in the most unexpected ways, at the most inopportune times. One time I was at a concert where Yasmeen was singing. One second, I was glowing with gratitude that she has grown into a strong, talented, thoughtful young person. The next thing I knew, I was thinking about Soraya not having that ability and was ugly crying. It is what it is.

Leena also struggles with expressing and verbalizing her feelings about the situation. She and Soraya are incredibly close and have "bestie sleepovers" six nights a week (I have let go of so many rules I used to think mattered). I even found out they have plans for playing jokes on people once Soraya has passed, going into fits of hysterical giggles about the pranks they are going to pull off. I suppose I should be grateful they can connect over this shared pain and make it funny.

Leena also has a difficult time detaching from home to go to school. Her heart is so divided, so torn. She fears something terrible will happen to Soraya while she's out in the world living her life, which manifests itself physically as headaches and stomachaches. She knows her body is processing her feelings somatically, but it doesn't make it any easier to get her out the door on a Monday. Some I just let her stay home. She's in third grade. She's not missing anything earth-shattering. I tell her emotional pain is just as legitimate a reason to stay home as a cold or flu.

She now always carries a cell phone with her because she feels she needs it in case of emergency. She uses it to watch Soraya's blood sugars throughout the day. She calls to talk to her sister from school, because if not, Soraya will already be asleep by the time she gets home from her activities. Without the context of our situation,

211

Landslide

there would have been zero reason I would have thought any third grader would need a cell phone. But she does, and I'm fine with it.

In general, Leena's way of dealing with her grief comes in the form of "I don't want to talk about it. I can't hear about it." Every now and then, though, she'll pipe up with questions like "What are we going to do with Soraya's bedroom after she's dead? Will we still be the Faruqui Five, or will we turn into the Faruqui Four?" I don't have adequate answers for her. Luckily, she agreed to see a therapist and try medication to help her process her thoughts and feelings more fully.

Leena has shared with us her complicated feelings about being on her new dance team. She loves performing but feels terrible that it takes time away from Soraya. Worse, Soraya desperately wants to dance as well and for obvious reasons cannot. "It makes me feel so guilty and bad," Leena cried to us.

"This is your thing," I assured her. "You need time and space away from the heaviness of this house. You deserve to be happy. Your life has to continue no matter what is happening at home."

"But I don't even know what I can do with Soraya to spend time with her anymore," Leena said. "There's so much she can't do."

The last of my preconceived notions of what it looks like to be a good pediatrician and parent fell away at that moment. "You know what, Leena?" I told her. "We've decided you don't have screen time limits on the weekend anymore. If you're not doing dance team and you've already finished your homework, you can sit on the couch with Soraya and watch a movie or play on your phone all day long."

On the other end of the spectrum is Yasmeen. She freely shares her feelings and expresses herself to us. She is frustrated and resentful about how hard things are for our family. She's not wrong. We give her space to be heard and respect her process.

Yasmeen feels no one at school could possibly relate to what she's going through and therefore has a difficult time making close friends. We try to let her know it isn't a competition and people can still empathize with her situation even if they haven't experienced it personally, but she finds very little comfort in that. She's in high school and my message to her now is that she'll find her people in college.

Whenever Yasmeen sees her friends stressing about getting a B on a test, she says, "I bet if Soraya wasn't here, you guys would be those kinds of parents who put pressure on me to get straight As." I'm not going to argue with that. It's possible. Who knows what those unentered sliding doors would have made of our lives.

"You'd probably make me go to the mosque every week, too," she continued.

I agreed with her. "Probably. That's something your dad really wanted." Although we talk about God and spirituality, life, and death all the time, the formal teachings of Islam have not been passed on to our girls in the way we would have liked.

Yasmeen has many regrets about her life. She feels she would be an entirely different person if Soraya was not in our family, and that may well be true. It's hard to know who any of us would be. The fact that Soraya exists has left an indelible mark on all our lives, and like life itself, it is simultaneously beautiful and terribly painful.

As for Soraya, she has so many things she wants to accomplish before her time on earth is up. She wants to start dating. She wants to experience her first kiss. She wants to get married. She wants to have a job. And if any of those things were available to her, I would tell her to go for it.

One day, Soraya said out of the blue, "I hate school."

It was a surprising statement. She's always loved school. I asked her why.

"Because I can't do anything!" she replied in frustration. "I want to take other classes. I want to stay for lunch and eat ice cream. I want to make friends, but I can't make friends if I'm not at school.

213

Landslide

I want homework. I don't even know anything in fifth grade, so how am I in sixth grade now?"

At that moment, I couldn't help but feel *Oh, I suck. Here I am bitching about my losses, and this girl has the insight to actually want homework.* I told her, "Soraya, if you want you can go to school full day."

"I'm so tired, Mom. My body can't do it," she said. "But I want to."

As a parent, I just wanted to fix it. But she was right. It was no longer within her capabilities. "Well, what if we got you worksheets to do?" I suggested.

Her eyes brightened up a bit. "Yes! And then if my hands got tired from writing, you guys could help me."

"Absolutely," I told her.

"What if we had no deadlines, too, so I never felt stressed about getting it done?" she suggested. "But I still want a grade."

"I'm sure we could make that happen."

"Great! I could take naps when I needed to and then do more work when I got up," she exclaimed. "That way, everyone will know I actually love school. I'm just mad that I can't do it."

Seeing as we were on a roll, I said, "What if I created a social group for you? I can talk to some other parents and make a schedule for peers to come see you, and that way you can make friends."

She said, "I would love that!"

The importance of social interaction is so ingrained in our human nature, and our family isn't enough to fill that need for her. We can give her Taylor Swift and Andy Grammer and swimming with dolphins, but she has been craving friendship with kids her own age.

Mostly, though, Soraya is struggling with the thought of dying. Contrary to her brave words when we first told her about her prognosis, she has a lot of fear about it. This is something that's on her mind, every day, nonstop, as it would be for any adult who was told their life was limited. She's thinking, *Where do I want to use my energy today? Where am I going to have the greatest impact?* Honestly, that's what we should all be doing.

We had to increase her antidepressant and antianxiety medications because she couldn't stop looking at cemeteries. She is now afraid of water because she thinks it might kill her. She's scared when we leave the house because she's worried we won't make it home before she dies. I keep telling her, "It's not happening today, and it's not happening tomorrow. We don't know when it's happening, but it's not happening now."

"My brain can't stop," she tells me. "All I can think about is not being here."

Fair enough. It was all I could think about, too.

Personal insight: Aside from having expectations of what my children would be like, I also had expectations of what type of parent I wanted to be. In being a pediatrician, I expected that I would follow all the current suggested guidelines. I so wanted to be a rule follower in this! However, Soraya's declining health and her need to have her blood sugar monitor on a cell phone are just a few examples of how that went out the window. My parenting perspective has shifted to simply meet my children where they are and what they need in our unique situation. Hence, Soraya and Leena have cell phones and no limits on screen time. I am my own worst critic, but I realize I have to take the judgment out of the equation.

Universal takeaway: There is *so much* judgment in how people parent and if they are following current guidelines in all sorts of topics from social media, screen time, breastfeeding, nutrition, and so on. Let's have more grace for each other and ourselves to trust that we are all doing the best we can and we certainly don't know everyone's circumstances.

Chapter 32

Take Me to Church

In times of crisis, people often turn to religion. Or they become disillusioned with formal expressions of faith and seek answers from a more spiritual realm. My feeling is whatever works is the thing to do. Or if none of it works, don't do any of it at all. Comfort can be found in many places.

Safi grew up in a very religious household, so when Soraya was first born, his parents thought more prayer was the solution to our problems. "Have you been praying five times a day? Did you fast for Ramadan?" Maybe they never said *this will get prayed away*, but that's how it felt at the time.

Today, Safi's parents still pray for Soraya, but the message is now one of surrender. It's *We will pray for her comfort. We will pray for your family. If this is how it is supposed to be and this is how it is, may this be easier for all of us.* Their view has evolved into something I find achingly beautiful, and I appreciate them far more than I ever would have believed possible. I see the way they love our kids, and it's just so pure. They have been compassionate, caring, and appropriately sad throughout our journey.

Safi also leans into his Islamic roots for comfort. One day, he announced, "I was talking to my therapist, and I realized I'm feeling out of control with how things are happening. I think it will make me feel better to talk to the Imam [Muslim spiritual leader] so I can learn what we have to do once Soraya passes." In our religion, you have to bury the body within twenty-four hours, and Safi is taking comfort in knowing the rites and rituals that will go along with that.

My mom seeks refuge in religion as well, but her version has always seemed more superstitious than factually derived to me. She prays five times a day and then she engages in an extra hour-and-a-half-long prayer at three in the morning. She seems to think this gives her extra credit with God. When it became apparent Soraya was declining, she took that to mean God was mad at her. She won't listen when she's told neither bonus prayer points nor God's wrath are what's causing Soraya's medical issues.

As for my dad, he finds himself questioning his faith these days. He can't understand why God would take Soraya. He says he doesn't know if he can go back to the mosque given the situation.

Soraya has also started looking to religion for answers. She had questions about dying that she wanted answered by an Imam, which we encouraged. He told her that when a child dies in Islam, they go straight to heaven, no questions asked. And then, when that child's parents die, the parents also get an automatic pass to heaven. She exclaimed, "Mom, that's my job—getting you guys into heaven!" This gave her some peace and a sense of purpose. Her willingness to sacrifice herself to save us was astounding and just another indication of her loving and generous nature.

Buoyed by her experience, I decided to talk to the Imam to answer some questions of my own, including *How does God make sense of a child's death?* He very kindly told me, "Soraya never belonged to you. You don't own her. You're her parents, but her soul belongs to God and that's where she will return." After that conversation, I thought, *What gives me the right to say God can't take her?* I found consolation in his explanation and now hold tightly to the idea that the Creator has a plan for her.

But the truth of the matter is I've decided religion is people-made. It is institutionalized moral guidance coupled with ceremonial

218

Keep Your Head Up

rituals to celebrate and mourn the big moments in our lives, and I'm good with all of that. But I also believe spirituality is our connection to truth, goodness, and light, and no one needs a church to access those things.

What I've learned from psychics, past life readers, and akashic guides over the past few years has offered me the same kind of peace that faith gives other people. While it may not fully align with traditional religion, I think that's okay. It's not like one has to be right and the other has to be wrong. Maybe they can both coexist peacefully.

These days, I rely on Mama Mary and other nontraditional sources to help me come to terms with Soraya's limited time left on earth. I feel like certain people are conduits of light, and they're tapping into the same thing religious people do but connecting and attuning to it in a different way. It's not religion per se, but it's certainly still acknowledging a higher power and forces greater than us.

Mama Mary speaks about white light, the creator, and guardian angels, which are all found in Islam. She was the first person outside of organized religion that made me realize there's something bigger connecting us. Mama Mary has been an incredible source of understanding and support since I was in college, and she is also mother to a special needs child who has since passed. She assures me she will be right by my side when Soraya moves on to another realm.

Another spiritual encounter with a past life reader helped ease my grief. He told me my soul is guided by a desire for immortality—that I want to leave a legacy and cause a beautiful ripple effect throughout the world. He said, "Life has kept throwing lemons. But not only do you turn it into lemonade, you transcend it in a way where you can truly help people."

This landed beautifully in my soul, because my inclination has always been to use my experience to help others. I'm trying, that's for sure, and I will keep right on trying. I never want anyone to feel as lost or as isolated as I have throughout this journey.

"And I am really sorry to say this," he added ever so gently, "but you can't be an expert on grief until you personally experience it. Sadly, this is the path you need to travel to become a teacher and healer for others."

This idea has become my guiding light. It is why I've started an online community for people experiencing anticipatory and other types of grief. It is why I am writing this book. I need to turn my pain into purpose. I need Soraya's life to be remembered and to matter.

Another message that really resonated with me came from a psychic at a wellness retreat. She had crystals scattered throughout her office, her hug was comforting, and she looked like a white light. She immediately relayed to me that Soraya is an angel.

"Her vibration is so strong, but her body is so weak," she told me. "She's making negotiations and will only go on her terms. If not, she'd already be gone."

Sounded accurate. I liked her vibe. I was willing to hear more.

"You have relatives who are ready for Soraya," she continued. "They are waiting for her."

Soraya had been telling us people on the other side were speaking to her. "Yes, they've been making themselves known," I told the psychic.

"She's not going to be able to go until you release her," she told me. "So please know that she's never going to leave you. You'll continue to communicate with each other. Notice the little things around you, because they will be her. Butterflies, birds . . ."

I tucked the thought away into my heart for somewhere down the line. Signs from Soraya would surely help the grief that awaited me. Some gray day in the future, I'd be looking for my daughter's spirit in the umber of a monarch's wing or dark feathers of a raven. I was overwhelmed with gratitude that day had not yet come.

"I'm not going to explain this any further, but please tell Soraya she can always come back home," she concluded, handing me a crystal elephant. "Give her this. She'll know what to do with it."

The next day, I gave Soraya the elephant and told her I'd gotten it from a woman who can connect with people who have passed away. She turned it over and over in her hands, considering it. "Mom, I want to talk to her," she finally said. "I want to know when I'm going to die."

"She says it's up to you," I replied.

Soraya's eyes lit up. "What?"

"She said you can decide when you go, and that you're negotiating it on your terms."

Soraya's bright eyes grew dark and stormy. "Well, I don't want to go. Ever."

"Then you don't have to," I said with a shrug. "She wanted me to tell you that all the things that you can't do here, you can do there. It's fun, but it's still your choice."

Soraya pondered this new information carefully. "So when do I need to decide? I can't decide right now!"

"You can decide whenever you want," I assured her. "But she said to tell you that you can always go home."

I found myself wondering if by "going home," the psychic meant Soraya will be able to connect with us—her family, her home—after she passes. Or was "home" heaven, where the spirits she says have been contacting her are? Is it where God lives? Is it the place we all come from and eventually return to, like the Imam told me?

As Soraya declines, it's interesting to hear about these more frequent encounters. She seems to have quite a strong connection to the other side, and it gives us all comfort knowing there are people there waiting to help her transition. She tells us, "I don't know who these people are, but they say they're our family and people who love us."

221

Take Me to Church

One night at dinner, she offhandedly commented that the guy I lived with as a child was very funny, but he smoked too much. That is the perfect description of my uncle, who took us in when my bio dad dumped us at his house. She also told us that one of Safi's friends has been holding her hand lately and telling her "it's fun over there." From her description, we can only believe she's talking to Safi's deceased medical partner, Dr. Hogan, who lived in Virginia and died two years ago.

She even channeled my best friend's father who had just passed. The words she used weren't ones she usually has in her vocabulary. The jokes were spot-on for him. Soraya even brought forth a message for my friend from her dad, which felt extremely apropos to the situation and helped bring her some closure.

Soraya tells me the spirits make a sound when they come in and out of her awareness. She feels their presence and the cadence of their voice when they arrive, and she hears a *whoosh* when they're leaving. She assumed we could hear these things too and was surprised to find out we do not.

I've told Soraya she is truly an angel, and the reason why she can connect with people on the other side is because she has a big purpose in life. She likes this idea and doesn't fear the spirits—she just takes it in stride. She has since learned what a medium is and has decided it is another job she wants to have before she leaves us.

Instead of being worried about these supernatural situations, all of us accept them. If this is paving the path for her to be greeted with unconditional love once she's on the other side, we're all for it. Who's to say what's real and what isn't?

As my dear cousin Julie likes to ponder, "Why can't it all be true?"

Personal insight: While I have always had my religion guide my beliefs in the afterlife, I craved wanting to know so much more when it came to Soraya. I wanted to know *why* and I wanted to learn from every explanation and every source I encountered. I was looking to give myself and Soraya some type of comfort. I don't think I would have sought out so many unconventional ways outside of traditional religion if it wasn't for Soraya. What did give me the most solace was between the Imam, psychics, and Soraya's channeling. The messages about what happens after death, the why, and purpose were all similar.

Universal takeaway: Keep the question open: why can't all religions and spiritual encounters have some overlapping elements of truth?

Chapter 33

Let Me In

When you have a child, you end up creating grand plans for their lives without even meaning to. You develop images of them playing with friends, going to their first sleepover, graduating high school and college, and following their passions and purpose. While these may never come to fruition under any circumstances, when you have a special needs child, the differences between your imaginings and reality are magnified even more. Very quickly you come to realize that the child you dreamed about—not on purpose and not on a conscious level—is not the child that you have in front of you, and it feels like death. You grieve who you thought you were birthing while adjusting to the beautiful child you were given.

There is no guidebook for how to do this. There is no charted path. It's a figure-it-out-as-you-go kind of thing.

While we were chasing a diagnosis during Soraya's early years, I found myself in the difficult position of conducting healthy child visits for all my patients. I could get through those exams, but after I'd have to sit in my office and sob. It's not that I wasn't happy for those children, but I couldn't help grieving that my child wasn't going to reach the same milestones on the same timeline, if ever.

Most parents I've met assume we have a lot in common when they find out we have a child the same age. While it's an understandable belief, it couldn't be farther from the truth, making an already isolating situation even more so. Parents of typical kids are usually concerned about ear infections, teething, potty training, making the

225

team, and getting into college. Meanwhile, families of special needs children are busy worrying about *will they ever walk? Will they ever verbally communicate? When will they die? Who's going to care for them after I die? How will I set up funds to take care of them?*

I was already used to being the outsider, so I simply stayed an outsider. Given the chaos at home, I wanted everything else to be as consistent and routine as possible. It was almost like I wanted the world to stop. I didn't let anyone new in, clinging to the people I already had in my life instead. My attitude was *I'm good. I'm not interested in new friends. I don't have time for it.* I thought the effort I was putting into my long-standing relationships was worth the work.

Still, I kept waiting for my circle—make that, who I thought was my circle—to step up. I had this narrative that people I had long-standing or blood relationships with were supposed to do certain things. When that didn't happen, I got really angry. I was convinced they owed me something, even when the universe kept showing me they weren't who or what I needed in those moments. I wasted so much time and energy thinking, *I need something from you and you're not doing it, so I'm frustrated with you.*

Now I simply believe people are doing the best they can. Sometimes that won't be enough. I can't force anyone to do anything, and if someone doesn't want to change, that's on them. These were hard realizations to accept, but so necessary for me to move forward in life.

I eventually learned my need for friendship, love, and understanding doesn't have to come from those few, select people I'd decided were my forever lifelines. It can also be fulfilled by people who truly want to play that role in my life and feel honored to do so. This is what makes a family.

To accept this new definition, I had to change my inner narrative. Before, whenever someone offered to help, I always wondered,

Are we worthy of that? It's not like these people are my parents or siblings or cousins or friends of several decades. They don't have to do anything for us! Now I know without a doubt that the answer is yes. Hell yes! Everyone deserves love.

I also used to wonder, *What do I have to give these people in return for their kindness and generosity? I know, I'll get them a gift card.* I never wanted to be vulnerable or accept help because it was too exhausting trying to figure out a repayment plan. I worried even more because I had no idea how much more help I'd need in the future. Would I be even more of a mess then? I didn't want to use up all the goodwill now, while Soraya was still with us.

Finally, I realized that like air, there's an unlimited quantity of unconditional love. I now gratefully accept meals from my neighbors every week. I know they feel good about helping us and don't want anything in return. I don't perseverate about paying back their kindness anymore—I just say thank you and feel happy they are in our lives.

Similarly, rather than shying away from new relationships, we've started adding friends like crazy. If we weren't going through what we are going through, I know for certain I wouldn't be searching for beautiful people to join us on our journey, but here we are. If people want to be part of us, we want them to be part of us.

We are now blessed by so many amazing friendships, many of which happened because of Soraya. Before, I never would have been open to asking the guy who works at Ulta for his phone number, no matter how great he seemed. Now, I'm letting my child text and FaceTime him and inviting him to our house for Sunday dinner. And guess what? He's awesome. Soraya picked up on his goodness right away. "Mom, he's going to love me for who I am. He's probably been bullied and feels different like I do, so we understand each other." How right she was.

To my surprise, these newer relationships never feel like work. They feel like magic. These *people* are magic, and I truly believe they are healing the part of me that always felt like I didn't fit in anywhere—because I fit in with them.

For the longest time, I talked about Soraya with a faraway face. I felt like I needed to hide our situation to protect other people's feelings. My excuse was it was too complicated, too draining, and I didn't want to deal with anyone's reactions.

I'd adopted a "say it, don't feel it" mentality. I told our story only to people who absolutely needed to know, mostly for my kids' benefit. Ironically, I usually ended up consoling the teacher or other significant adult who was learning about our situation rather than the other way around. *Please stop crying,* I'd always think. *Don't you know I'm the one who's supposed to be crying?*

But I realized that speaking about our experience helps me affect more people. I ripped that bandage off and started an Instagram page to share our story and provide support for other parents of medically complex children and those with a limited life span. I've been buoyed by the comments from the people who can see Soraya clearly through my writing. *She's a bright light. She's an angel. She's such an old soul.* It has also surprised me how many people were heartbroken by our situation. Not to be dramatic, but it pretty much restored my faith in humanity.

I'm slowly peeling away layers that covered me for so long. It feels so liberating, like laying down a burden. I may be imperfect and broken, but I'm trying as hard as I can—just like everyone else.

We are all human, floundering around in our own humanity. Sometimes we succeed and sometimes we fail. But I'm here to catch anyone who is falling into that deep dark hole, and I now know there are plenty of people willing to do that for me as well.

It feels like a miracle.

Personal insight: I had the belief that my long-standing relationships and family were supposed to do certain things for me. When that didn't happen, I wasted so much time and energy thinking about it and being angry.

I also had this wild belief that since I had great friends already, I felt that any new friendships would take too much energy. I learned that when you let people who *want* to be in your life in, it doesn't require much work. It's effortless and enhances your life in a magical way. Soraya has been the greatest teacher in finding the most beautiful people.

Universal takeaway: When you are going through something *really* tough over a long period of time, it may not be enough for certain people in your family to recognize it or help. The world, and specifically your family, doesn't owe you anything for your hardship.

However, let those people in who want to be in your life. It's never too late to make a new friend. Your heart doesn't have a capacity for the amount of love you can have for others and how much you can receive.

Chapter 34

Another Life

Every so often, I like to hold what I call the Babysitters Club. I get as many of our caregivers together for a party to thank them for being such an integral part of our lives. On this occasion, one of them brought each of my girls a sunflower in a mason jar as a hostess gift.

A week later, Soraya was staring at the flowers intently, one of which wasn't faring so well. She asked me, "Whose flower is the one that's dying?"

"I don't know," I replied, fearing it would be hers.

"Just tell me what name is on it," Soraya demanded.

"Honestly, honey, it doesn't matter," I told her, hoping she'd just drop the subject.

Soraya went and looked. "It's mine," she said, her eyes filling with tears. "Yasmeen and Leena's sunflowers are so happy, but mine isn't."

Reminders of the circle of life seem to be everywhere we look these days. Now even the cut stems of a simple floral arrangement are telling the same sad story. Sunflowers are serving as a reminder of what lies ahead.

We meet with Dr. Meyer every few weeks instead of twice a year these days. The last time we had an appointment, he asked me, "How are you doing with Soraya's rapid decline?"

It's not that I don't realize her health is deteriorating—we had to make three vent changes and increase her medications several times in the past month. But for whatever reason, it felt different hearing the words spoken out loud. His question sent me into a panic.

Am I in denial? I wondered. *Am I not looking at this the right way? Am I not being hopeful if I believe this?*

Despite knowing an answer will never come, I am still desperate for clarity. We may never know *why* this all happened, so now I've shifted to wanting to know *when* it will happen. But as wonderful as Dr. Meyer is, he's not God. My guess is as good as his.

I've always been a planner. As much as I hate to admit it now, when Soraya came along, I felt she was a barrier to the plans I had for my medical career. I kept thinking about all the jobs that I couldn't have because of her. I had issues with people knowing I had a daughter with special needs. For some reason, I felt it would make me appear incapable of taking care of their children if I was barely keeping my own child alive.

However, I've realized all the things my patients love about me have very little to do with my technical skills and a whole lot to do with my experience being Soraya's mother. I've learned more about being a pediatrician from her than I ever did in school. It's apparent in the amount of patience I display with families. The time I spend with them. The fact that I care enough to ask parents how *they* are doing. The experience I share when advocating for their children with special needs.

I thought Soraya was getting in the way of my career, but I had it all backwards. My superpower of being a great pediatrician is *because* of her. This isn't a natural talent; it's an acquired talent from being Soraya's mother.

I used to think once Soraya leaves this earth, I'd simply shift back to where I always thought my life should have been headed. I am now realizing that's not where I want to go anymore. We all grow and change through our life experiences, and this one will never allow me to return to who I once was.

In a life I've always tried to control, my lesson is now one of surrender. I have to release the illusion of control, which in reality never existed in the first place. Things will take shape in whatever way they choose, in whatever time feels right. Acceptance is my only option.

Although I still can't imagine what life will be like when Soraya's gone, I cannot and will not lie down and die with her. I have two other children, and I don't want their lives to stop. I know they, too, will be forever changed by this experience, but I'm also absolutely convinced we will all survive this. We have to. There's no other choice.

I'm sure we'll be in a rebuilding phase, for who knows how long, and I don't even care what lies ahead for us. All I know is it will be a bigger plan than my plan ever was. I'm willing to follow the trail of breadcrumbs leading me in another direction and have faith I will end up exactly where I'm meant to be.

I'm not saying any of this happened for a reason, because I loathe that trite phrase. What I am saying is that this path has readied me for my true purpose. I would not have been able to see it unless my heart was open—and all that took was having everything I thought I ever wanted and needed ripped away from me.

Today, I no longer try to force life in a certain direction. I simply try to soak in whatever time we have left together and enjoy every second. I know there is still wonder around every corner, in moments where I least expect it.

One day, we were hanging out in the kitchen as a family listening to the Andy Grammer station on Pandora. Suddenly, the volume went from softly sweet to club-level loud, and no one had touched a button or asked Siri to do it. We all looked at each other in surprise.

233

Another Life

"Oh, that's just Dr. Hogan," Soraya told us nonchalantly, referencing Safi's medical partner who died a few years back and has been one of the spirits coming to Soraya regularly. "He wants you to listen to the message. He knows you're stressed."

The song was one we all know well—"Good to Be Alive (Hallelujah)." We all started laughing and singing along.

Feels good to be alive right about now
Good, good, good, good to be alive right about now
Good, good, good, good to be alive right about now
Hallelujah

After that, the dance party continued with Andy's "Keep Your Head Up." Typically, Pandora doesn't play the same artist back to back. I guess Dr. Hogan had different thoughts.

Later, Soraya gave me a hug for longer than normal and told me, "I don't want to lose you. Remember, I get to decide when I go."

Whenever that time comes, I'm praying all the angels, uncles, family friends, and pets are there to greet her with loving arms. I know she'll give them the kind of hugs I'll be missing forever. And until we meet again, I hope to see her as often as possible on butterflies' wings and in black-feathered birds.

Personal insight: Throughout this book you have seen so many beliefs that I had that I hung onto. These beliefs revolved around dreams that I couldn't let go of. I was so determined to control my future. I believe if I changed the course that I had failed. I also felt that if I had so many bad things happen to me that I would reach a limit and no more challenges could happen.

In reality all of the challenges that I encountered throughout my life were a training program. These obstacles gave me the coursework to become Soraya's mother. In return she has been the greatest teacher. I look back when I thought her medical condition was a hindrance to my career. Everything I have learned by being her mother has made me the best pediatrician I can be. My superpowers of compassion were not something that could be taught.

Universal takeaway: Sometimes you may learn your best lessons from having the toughest struggles. When your biggest fears turn into your reality, it is then we must surrender, as you have nothing left to lose. Surrendering and trusting that there is something greater than ourselves may be the most beautiful gift you can give to yourself.

Conclusion: Take This Ride

"Welcome to Holland" is a short but powerful poem written by Emily Perl Kingsley, a mother and writer. It's often shared by parents of children with disabilities because of how beautifully it captures the unexpected journey, the grief of changed expectations, and the quiet joy found in a different kind of life.

When I first read this poem, it was like someone had finally put words to the swirl of emotions I was carrying. Navigating the unexpected path of raising a child with special needs, I often felt isolated—like everyone else was speaking a language I didn't understand, living in a place I couldn't reach. I couldn't find my people, the ones who truly *got it*. This poem helped me feel seen in a time where I didn't know any other families that I could connect to. It reminded me that while my journey might look different, it's still meaningful, beautiful, and filled with its own kind of wonder. It gave me comfort, perspective, and most important, the sense that I wasn't alone.

I'd like to share it with you now. As you read, I would like to ask you: have you ever had a life experience that didn't go as planned, but still brought unexpected beauty or growth? If so, I know this poem will resonate with you.

Welcome to Holland
by Emily Perl Kingsley
Copyright©1987 by Emily Perl Kingsley.
All rights reserved.

Reprinted by permission of the author.

I am often asked to describe the experience of raising a child with a disability—to try to help people who have not shared that unique experience to understand it, to imagine how it would feel. It's like this . . . . . .

When you're going to have a baby, it's like planning a fabulous vacation trip—to Italy. You buy a bunch of guide books and make your wonderful plans. The Coliseum. The Michelangelo David. The gondolas in Venice. You may learn some handy phrases in Italian. It's all very exciting.

After months of eager anticipation, the day finally arrives. You pack your bags and off you go. Several hours later, the plane lands. The flight attendant comes in and says, "Welcome to Holland."

"Holland?!?" you say. "What do you mean Holland?? I signed up for Italy! I'm supposed to be in Italy. All my life I've dreamed of going to Italy."

But there's been a change in the flight plan. They've landed in Holland and there you must stay.

The important thing is that they haven't taken you to a horrible, disgusting, filthy place, full of pestilence, famine and disease. It's just a different place.

So you must go out and buy new guide books. And you must learn a whole new language. And you will meet a whole new group of people you would never have met.

It's just a different place. It's slower-paced than Italy, less flashy than Italy. But after you've been there for a while and you catch your breath, you look around . . . .. and you begin to notice that Holland has windmills . . . .. and Holland has tulips. Holland even has Rembrandts.

But everyone you know is busy coming and going from Italy . . . and they're all bragging about what a wonderful time they had there. And for the rest of your life, you will say "Yes, that's where I was supposed to go. That's what I had planned."

And the pain of that will never, ever, ever, ever go away . . . because the loss of that dream is a very very significant loss.

But . . . if you spend your life mourning the fact that you didn't get to Italy, you may never be free to enjoy the very special, the very lovely things . . . about Holland.

Acknowledgments

This book would not exist without the support, encouragement, and belief of so many incredible people.

To Trish Cook and the amazing team at KAA—thank you for championing this project from day one. Trish, a special thank you for your creativity and the deep connection you brought to both me and this book. Your insight and heart left a lasting imprint on every page.

To Courtney—thank you for your continued creativity, encouragement, and support throughout this journey.

Deep gratitude to Nena Madonia Oshman and Kelly Young at The Nominate Group—thank you for saying *yes* to me and for helping this book find its perfect home. To Amy Fandrei—thank you for seeing something in this story before it was a book.

To the incredible team at Wiley, and to the best editor a writer could hope for—Sunnye—thank you for your steady hand, thoughtful edits, and unwavering commitment to this story.

To all those who encouraged this nudge to write: Lori Mulady Burdick, Mia, Amir, Anna, Steve, Kristi, Tony, Mary Carol, and Devin—thank you for being part of the foundation that held me up. And to the crew who walked with me through every single step—Julie, Tim, Mark, and Sarah—your presence and support were everything.

To Dr. Olivia, Mama Mary, and Ainslie—thank you for your wisdom, grounding guidance, and the light you brought to my path. Your presence helped me navigate both the writing process and the life behind it with greater clarity and grace.

A special thank-you to the mother authors who extended their wisdom, time, and hearts: Kelly Cervantes, Jessica Fein, and Myra Sacks—your generosity and solidarity helped light the way.

My deepest gratitude goes to my husband, Safi—thank you for believing in this wild idea from the very beginning and for standing beside me every step of the way. To my parents—your love and encouragement made this possible.

And finally, to my heart and soul: Yasmeen, Soraya, and Leena. Being your mother made me a writer. Without you, there would be no story to tell.

About the Author

Dr. Tasha Faruqui is a practicing pediatrician who lives in Cincinnati, Ohio, with her husband, Safi, their three daughters—Yasmeen, Soraya, and Leena—two cats (Prince and Ohana), and their beloved therapy dog, Taco. A graduate of the University of Michigan, she earned her medical degree from the Arizona College of Osteopathic Medicine and completed her pediatric residency through the University of Toledo and Cincinnati Children's Hospital.

Inspired by her father, a physician and surgeon who served the rural community of Dowagiac, Michigan, Tasha joined the National Health Service Corps after medical school with the intention of continuing his legacy. That path changed when her second daughter, Soraya, was born with a rare, still-undiagnosed medical condition. This personal journey shifted Tasha's focus toward pediatric care, with a deep commitment to advocacy for families of medically complex children, especially those with limited life expectancy.

She has practiced pediatrics in Portsmouth, Virginia, and Cincinnati, Ohio. Today, she shares a message of fierce and loving hope with medical students at Cincinnati Children's Hospital, at Make-A-Wish events, and through her online community (@thefaruqui5). Tasha was named a Top Doctor by *Cincinnati Magazine* in 2022, 2024, and 2025. Learn more at www.tashafaruqui.com.

Index

A

Abandonment, feelings, 151
Acceptance, metaphor, 103
Acting out, 9
Advanced maternal age, 67, 123
Aging parents, child
    responsibility, 135
A-ha moment, 142
Alternative healing methods,
    research, 23–24
Americanization, 5
American lifestyle, living, 6
Anesthesia, response, 148, 149
Anti-cancer/anti-inflammatory
    medications, usage
    (suggestion), 154
Anxiety, 151
  feeling, 156
Arranged marriage, 17
  agreement, 33
  completion, 4–5
  consideration, 3–4, 48
Aspiration, 82–83
Assimilation, 5

B

Babies, genetic anomaly
    (increase), 123
Babysitters Club, 231
Biomechanics, 14
Blood
  sugar, levels (problem), 138–139,
    149–150, 177–178
  work, 175
Bone density, building, 116
Borderline jaundice, 130–131
Breastfeeding, 69–71, 73, 130–131
  continuation, 77
  desire, 124
  issues, 58, 66
Breath, shortness, 157

C

Care conference, medical team
    involvement, 154
Career
  discussion, 36–37
  parenthood, balance
    (difficulty), 66

Caregiver
  grandmother, role (cessation), 128
  interview, 74
  problems, 75–76
Caregiver, search, 73
Cat
  feline intestinal peritonitis (FIP), 187–188
  purchase, 181–182
Center of Excellence (Cincinnati Children's Hospital), 138–139
Chest muscles, problems, 161
Childcare, absence, 7
Child psychiatry, rotations, 52
Children
  attention, considerations, 131
  disability, raising (description), 238–239
  firstborn. *See* Firstborn.
  secondborn. *See* Secondborn.
  suffering, expectations, 123
  thirdborn. *See* Thirdborn.
Children with special needs, pediatric care, 128–129
Chronic sleep deprivation, 113–114
Cincinnati Bengals, attendance, 205

Cincinnati Children's
  doctors/therapists, search, 137–140
  Grammer, appearance, 197–198
  job acceptance/opportunity, 134–135
Cincinnati, family (move), 137
Cognitive ability, problem, 141
Community
  friendliness/family orientation, 5–6
  outliers, 6–7
  place, finding (struggle), 11–12
Computed tomography (CT) scan, 158
Concerts, attendance, 206–207
Coping skills, 145
COVID, impact, 155, 175–176
Cranial-sacral therapy, 23
C-section, consideration, 68, 130
Cultural transition, difficulty, 4
Culture, discussion, 11

D
Daycare, 73
  concerns, 77
  limitations, 108
  search, 59
  usage, 77

Death
  approach/explanation, 198–203, 209
  clarity, search, 232
  decision, 220–221
Depression/confusion, 22–23
  escape, 27–28
Disney World/Universal trip, 205
Doctor of Osteopathy (DO)
  applicant well-roundedness, importance, 14
  becoming, 23
  holistic clinician role, consideration, 14
  impact, 13

E

Echocardiogram, 175
Education
  expectations, pressure, 21
  requirement/importance, 2–3
End-tidal CO_2 monitor, observation, 161
Energy work, 23
Epidural, option, 130
Ergonomics, 14
Exhaustion, increase, 163
Expectations (life theme), 1
Experiences, speaking/explanation, 228

F

Failures, impact, 21
Failure to thrive, diagnosis, 77–78, 83–84
Family
  cat, purchase, 181–182
  chaos/routine, 144
  constitution, 226
  disruption, G tube (impact), 100–101
  Hawaii, trip, 177–179
  management, 58
  rebuilding phase, anticipation, 233
  Safi, sacrifice, 110–111
  survival mode, 102–103
Faruqui Five, performance, 198
Father
  medical issues, 41–44
  recovery/softness, 45–46, 50
  sepsis (blood infection), 44–45
  sibling responsibility, 105
Fatigue, increase, 157, 169
Fear
  impact, 117, 177
  increase, 214–215
Feeding schedule, flexibility, 139
Feeding therapy
  continuation, 115
  difficulties, 83, 87
  need, 81
  problems, 108–109

247

Index

Fertility, issues/fears, 52–53

Fierce independence (life theme), 1

Fight, flight, or freeze (reactions), 90

Financial insecurity, fear, 156

Fine motor skills, improvement, 97

Firstborn (Yasmeen)

abandonment, feelings, 151

attention, need, 97

coping, assistance (need), 151

crankiness/irritableness, 101

ease, 59–60

future, parental dreams, 60

Grammer concert, 188–189

grief, 212–213

hospital visit, return (avoidance), 150

life, unfairness, 173–174, 184

misery, 106

overachiever/adaptability, 96

self-loathing, 151

sibling experience, desire, 123

struggles, 100–101

vomiting, 148

Fitting in (life theme), 1

Flonase, usage, 157

Friendship/relationship, dysfunction, 20–22, 29

G

Gait

change, 153

problem, 147–148

Gastro-intestinal (GI) rotation, 88

Gender, discussion, 11

Genetic anomaly, increase, 123

Genetic counseling, career, 17–18

Genetic tests, continuation, 114–115

Graduate school, issues, 19–20

Grammer, Andy (concerts/meeting), 188–189, 197–198, 206–208

Grief

ease, 219–220

online community, 220

presence, 209–211, 225

Gross motor sklls, focus, 97

Group homes, discussion/consideration, 142–143

Growth chart, problems, 77–78, 89

G tube

checking, 158–159

feeding, 99–100, 177

feeds, increase, 97

placement, 97

replacement, desire, 105

schedule, impact, 100–101

supplies, requirements, 99
surgery, 93, 95–96
tubing, attachment
    (psychological effect),
    107
usage, 89–90, 92, 139

H

Head lag, absence (timing), 78
Hemophagocytic
    lymphohistiocytosis
    (HLH) specialist, 154
High-risk OB personnel,
    involvement, 129
High school experience,
    absence, 10
Hogan, Chris, 110
Hospice. *See* Starshine
    Hospice
Hospital, rotations, 50–51
Husband, future, 40
Hyperextension, appearance, 147
Hyperventilation, 90
Hypoventilation, symptoms, 162

I

Illnesses, normalization, 77
Immortality, desire, 219
Inadequacies, overthinking, 22–23
Inner narrative, change,
    226–227
Insomnia, 151

Insurance company
    approval, 121
    denial, 115, 117–118
Islamic roots, comfort, 217–218

J

Job
    enjoyment, 17, 205, 209
    part-time work
        schedule, accommodation,
        133
        search, 133–134
    search, 132–133
    uncertainty, 156

K

Kingsley, Emily Perl, 237

L

Laryngeal cleft, 94
    absence, 97
Leena. *See* Thirdborn
Letters of recommendation,
    usage, 62
Life
    balance, 27
    challenge, 6–7
    control, regaining, 92
    direction, acceptance, 233
    joy, reduction, 173–174
    mourning, 239
    performance, pressure, 59

Life (*continued*)
quitting, desire, 21
stressors, 14
transformation, 25
Long-term relationships,
development, 17
Love language, 6

M
Macrophages, diseases, 154
Magnetic resonance imaging
(MRI), obtaining, 84,
147–148, 175
Make-A-Wish, grant/trip, 177,
181, 205
Malignant hyperthermia, 148
Malnutrition
cause, 83–84
cure, 93–94
Mama Mary, 12, 24, 44
advice, 117, 135
job search, assistance, 134–135
reliance, 219
warning, 125
Maternal fetal medicine
personnel, involvement,
129
Maternity leave, cessation,
58–59
Math/science camp, attendance,
10
Mayo Clinic, consultation, 154

Medical problems (cause),
knowledge (absence),
118
Medical reassurance, 87
Medical school, rotations, 38, 41
Medication, fear (stigma), 156
Medicine
hierarchy, 85
holistic approach, 15
Mental health, management, 21
Mentorship, 41
Military deployment, 40
Miscarriage-54, 53
Mitochondrial disease
cause, possibility, 121–122
detection, 114
result, abnormalities, 154
treatment, 153
Motherhood
expectations/reality, contrast,
58
firstborn, ease, 59–60
issues/fears, 52–53
Muscle biopsy, 153, 177
insurance company approval,
121
negative result, 125, 127
surgery, pain, 122
usage, consideration, 114–115
Muscles
control, absence, 71
electromyography, 175

250
Index

strength, issues, 116, 175
tone, problem, 115
weakness, 165, 169
Muscular dystrophies,
determination, 114

N
Nanny cam, usage, 74–75
Nasogastric (NG) tube, usage,
89–90
failure, 93
National Health Service Corps
(NHSC)
commitment, 39, 65–66
cessation, approach, 131
fulfillment, 101, 108
continuation, 61
qualifying practice,
acceptance, 66
Scholarship, compliance, 52
National Institutes of Health
(NIH), referral/
appointment/assistance,
163–164, 165, 175, 176
Neonatal intensive care unit,
usage, 69
Neurotypical sibling, desire, 113

O
Obstetrics/gynecology, rotations,
51–52
Occupational therapy

continuation, 115
need, 81, 97
Osteopathy, curiosity, 13
Overthinking, 156, 182
Oxygen exchange, assistance,
165

P
Pain
control, 170
Tylenol, usage, 155
Palliative care, 182–183
appointment, 171–172
consideration, 169–171
Panic attack, 156
Parenthood
careers, balance (difficulty),
66
concerns, medical dismissal
(impact), 85
genetic counseling, 95
Parent-teacher conference, 141
Part-time work
schedule, accommodation, 133
search, 133–134
Patients
communication, change, 85
long-lasting bonds, 18
specialist, referral, 86
PediaSure, usage, 139
Pediatricians
talent, acquisition, 232–233

Pediatricians, reassurance/
validation (role), 85
Pediatrics
residency, transfer, 61–63
rotations, initiation, 50–51
Personality changes, 161–162
Personal struggles, viewpoint,
32–33
Physical therapy
continuation, 115
goal, 109
need, 81, 97
Physician, listening skills, 148
Pneumonia, 77, 82
Politics, discussion, 11
Potty training, 144
Praying, 217
Pregnancy
experience, 53–55, 127–131
firstborn, 57–58
labor, 57
logistics, 124
self-imposed time limit, 127
termination, consideration
(clarity), 124
Premature babies, appearance,
140
Privacy, invasion, 75
Problem-solving skills, usage,
48–49
Proposal, parental permission, 39
Psychological stressors, 14

Public schools, attendance, 141
Pulmonary function testing, 175

Q
Quality of life, improvement
(desire), 117–118

R
Race, discussion, 11
Rainbow Babies, muscle biopsy
expense, 115, 118
insurance company approval,
121
Reassurance mode, 157
Recessive gene, impact
(possibility), 114–115
Reflux problems, 71, 82, 116
Reiki, 23
Relationships, perception, 228
Religion
discussion, 11
perception, 218–219
refuge, 218
understanding, 7
Residency
interview, 62–63
placements, 28
Rotations, 50–52, 88
clinical setting, 38–39
continuation, 49
exploration, 38
med school setting, 41

Ruland, Rob (Afghanistan deployment), 110

S

Safi
  Afghanistan deployment, 84, 109
    replacement, 110
  breakup, opinion, 35–36
  calmness, 46
  Doctor of Osteopathy (DO), 61–62
  meeting, 29–33
  mentor, contact, 133
  Navy deferment, 54
  Navy deployment, 61, 65
  panic attacks, 156
  parents, religiosity (strictness), 48–49
  reenlistment, option (absence), 124
  relationship
    considerations, 37–39
    continuation, 37–38
  SSRI, usage, 157
  surgery fellowship interviews, 60–61
  vasectomy, consideration, 94
School
  importance, 2–3
  quitting, 22
  return, 27

Secondborn (Soraya), 66–69
  active decline, observation (parental panic), 156
  appointments, scheduling, 137
  aspiration, 82–83
  behavioral issues, absence, 141–142
  blood sugar, issues, 138–139, 149–150, 177–178
  bone density, building, 116
  breathing problems, 158–159
  breath, shortness, 157
  chest muscles, problems, 161
  chest walls, weakening (potential), 163
  complications, 68–71
  computed tomography (CT) scan, 158
  coordination, absence, 78
  daycare, limitations, 108
  death, approach/explanation, 198–203, 209
  ER stabilization, 149
  exercises, repetitions, 155
  exhaustion, increase, 163, 175
  failure to thrive, diagnosis, 77–78, 83–84
  fatigue, increase, 157, 169
  fear, increase, 214–215
  feeding
    difficulties, 83, 87
    need, 81

253
Index

Secondborn (Soraya)
(*continued*)
   schedule, flexibility, 139
   therapy, problems, 108–109
fine motor skills,
   improvement, 97
firstborn love/hatred/
   resentment, 150–151
fussiness, 70–71
future, consideration, 142–144
gait
   change, 153
   problem, 147–148
gross motor skills, focus, 97
group homes, discussion/
   consideration, 142–143
G tube, usage. *See* G tube.
head control/strength,
   problem, 78
head lag, 78
health status, care (options),
   132
hyperextension, appearance,
   147
illnesses, frequency, 87, 101
irritability, continuation, 169
laryngeal cleft, 94
   absence, 97
magnetic resonance imag-
   ing (MRI), obtaining, 84,
   147–148
malignant hyperthermia, 148

malnutrition
   cause, 83–84
   cure, 93
medical history, complexity,
   132, 137
medical mystery, 125
milestones, missing, 113
mitochondrial disease, 114,
   121–122
   result, abnormalities, 154
   treatment, 153
muscles
   biopsy, 114–115, 121–122,
   125–127, 177
   control, absence, 71
   strength, issues, 116, 175
   tone, problem, 115
muscular incoordination, 87
nutritional needs, 101
pain
   constancy, 87
   control, 170
   Tylenol, usage, 155
personality changes, 161–162
pneumonia, 77, 82
potty training, 144
public preschool experience,
   141
quality of life, improvement
   (desire), 117–118
reflection point, 143
reflux problems, 71, 82, 116

regressions, 115–116

school, difficulty (increase), 213–215

sensory issues, 150

sippy cup, usage, 116

sip ventilator, usage, 210

sleep apnea, Flonase treatment, 157

sleep study, 157–158

  results, 161

special needs, 141–142

spinal muscular atrophy (SMA), 83

spirits, channeling, 221–222

stander, usage, 116–117

surgery, pain, 121, 162

swallow study, 81–82

sweating, 83

terminal diseases, tests, 94

therapy

  expense, 133

  need, 81

thirdborn, doctor/patient (playing), 158–159

tiredness, 69–70

tone, issues, 69–71, 83–84

tracheostomy

  decision/refusal, 193–195

  privacy, invasion, 191–192

  usage, 163, 166, 170, 191

ventilator, necessity/usage, 162–166, 169, 176

walking, learning, 116

weight gain, absence, 77, 84, 87

X-rays, usage, 82

Self-care, 145

  impossibility, 107–108

  time allotment, need, 106

Sensory issues, 150

Serotonin reuptake Inhibitor (SSRI), usage, 156–157

Sexuality, discussion, 11

Sippy cup, usage, 116

Sip ventilator, usage, 210

Sleep apnea, Flonase treatment, 157

Sleep study, 157–159, 162

  results, 161

Soraya. *See* Secondborn

  sleeplessness, 101–102

Specialist, referral, 86

Special needs children, sibling empathy (assumption), 150

Speech therapy

  continuation, 115

  improvements, 109

  need, 81

Spinal muscular atrophy (SMA), 83

Stander, usage, 116–117

Starshine Hospice, joining, 182–183

Steroid trials, usage (suggestion), 154

Strayed, Cheryl, 103

Stress
feeling, 156
presence, 144
reduction, 131
Swallow study, 81–82

T
Terminal diseases, tests, 94
Therapy
consideration, 106–107
return, 144–145
usage, impossibility, 107–108
Thirdborn (Leena)
borderline jaundice, 130–131
breastfeeding, 130–131
doctor/patient playing, 158–159
grief, 211
pregnancy/birth, 127–131
Tiny Beautiful Things (Strayed), 103
Tone, issues, 69–71, 83–84
Tracheostomy, 191
consideration, 163, 166, 170, 172
decision/refusal, 193–195
privacy, invasion, 191–192
Trauma pager, usage, 148–149
Trust, establishment, 107

U
Ultrasound
due dates, accuracy, 67
images, normalcy, 129
Unconditional love, 227

V
Ventilator, necessity/usage, 162–166, 169, 176

W
Walking, learning, 116
Wedding
completion, 49
compromise, 49
postponement, discussion, 47–48
scheduling, 40, 41
Weight gain, absence, 77, 84, 87
"Welcome to Holland" (Kingsley), 237–238
Wild (Strayed), 103
Women, reproductive health (research), 24
Work
ethic, 62
mental health day, 91
transition/guilt, 59
Worrying, continuousness, 156

X
X-rays, usage, 82

Y
Yasmeen. *See* Firstborn